D1117267

The Newspaper Survival Book

An Editor's Guide to
Marketing Research / PHILIP MEYER

THE
NEWSPAPER
SURVIVAL
BOOK

INDIANA UNIVERSITY PRESS • BLOOMINGTON

WITHDRAWN
FROM
UNIVERSITY OF PENNSYLVANIA
LIBRARIES

Z
286
N48
M49
1985

Portions of the following chapters have appeared elsewhere in slightly different form:
Chapter 3: *presstime*, Copyright 1982, American Newspaper Publishers Association.
Chapter 4: *Journalism Quarterly*, Copyright 1978, Association for Education in Journalism and Mass Communications.
Chapter 5: *Newspaper Research Journal*, Copyright 1980, Association for Education in Journalism and Mass Communications.
Chapter 7: *ANPA News Research Report No. 34*, Copyright 1982, American Newspaper Publishers Association.
Chapter 9: *ANPA News Research Report No. 24*, Copyright 1979, American Newspaper Publishers Association.
Chapter 12: *IEEE Journal on Selected Areas in Communications*, Copyright 1983, The Institute of Electrical and Electronic Engineers, Inc.

Copyright © 1985 by Philip Meyer

All rights reserved

No part of this book may be reproduced or utilized in any form
or by any means, electronic or mechanical, including photocopying
and recording, or by any information storage and retrieval system,
without permission in writing from the publisher. The Association
of American University Presses' Resolution on Permissions constitutes
the only exception to this prohibition.

Manufactured in the United States of America

Library of Congress Cataloging in Publication Data

Meyer, Philip.
  The newspaper survival book.

  Bibliography: p.
  Includes index.
  1. Newspapers—Marketing.   2. Newspaper publishing.
3. Marketing research.   I. Title.   II. Title: Editor's
guide to marketing research.
Z286.N48M49   1985   070'.68'8   84-48042
ISBN 0-253-15835-4
1 2 3 4 5 89 88 87 86 85

UNIVERSITY
OF
PENNSYLVANIA
LIBRARIES

For Hilda

Contents

Preface

Running a newspaper used to be a lot simpler. Before the competition for readers' time and money made a marketing orientation necessary, newspapers were a lot like public utilities. Managers had a fairly standard product to create, and the need for it was so basic that readers would be loyal so long as the production and distribution process kept putting it out there for them to buy. Management never had to think about the market at all, but could concentrate instead on the elements of the process: keeping the organization staffed, controlling costs, monitoring service. Looking back from today's market-oriented environment, that seems like pretty easy work. The number of variables on the production side is limited, they are easy to measure, and their effects are predictable. When the nature of the product is never questioned, management decisions deal mainly with getting it out the gate in the cheapest and easiest manner.

The need for marketing has changed all that. The audience is fickle and the product no longer a given. Those making managerial decisions are forced to consider many more variables, and the outcomes are no longer so easy to predict. Newspapers, sometimes begrudgingly, have become entrepreneurial companies defining themselves less in terms of the product and more in terms of the needs of their customers. Discovering those needs and responding with product innovations have become complicated and challenging tasks. And they have introduced a disturbing level of uncertainty into the managerial environment.

Reduction of that uncertainty is the task of market research. I entered the field very tentatively in 1969 when the *Charlotte Observer* asked me to take some time off from my duties as a Washington correspondent for the Knight newspapers to run a survey of its market. Some of the advice that project produced—pay more attention to television, give greater consideration to the information needs of the black population—turned out to be pretty good. As concern for shrinking newspaper penetration grew, I was detailed to more marketing projects and eventually wound up in Miami on the corporate staff of what was by then Knight-Ridder Newspapers, Inc. Part of the task was to learn how businesses with traditional marketing orientations solved their problems and see what of their technology might be adapted to newspaper research.

Two aphorisms from the literature of technological transfer appear to apply here. One is that technology is transferred more by agents than by agencies. The other says that it is easier to buy technology than to use it. In the newspaper field, there was no shortage of market researchers, themselves good examples of entrepreneurship, who were ready with exotic techniques to apply to editorial decision making. But where they succeeded, it was not the cleverness of the technique that mattered so much as the ability to ignite a spark of communication between editor and researcher. No one has figured out how to institutionalize that spark. In its absence, a lot of technology is bought but unused—or used below its potential.

The purpose of this book is to improve communication between newspaper managers and researchers by explaining how the research process works and providing some examples of research that helps—or could help, with more development. This is a field in which diffusion of innovation is hampered by the proprietary nature of some of the most interesting and innovative work. If more work were shared—both the successes and the failures—the field could develop more quickly. Fortunately, the management of Knight-Ridder has permitted and even encouraged publication of the results of many of the experimental studies undertaken during my time there. I am especially grateful to Lee Hills and Derick J. Daniels, who got me started on the marketing problem, and to James K. Batten and Alvah H. Chapman, Jr., who provided a corporate environment where untested ideas could be examined and tried. Parts of this manuscript were reviewed and commented on by Albert E. Gollin, Les Bogart, Mark Appelbaum, David Weaver, Stuart Tolley, Virginia Dodge Fielder, John Koslick, and Frederick C. Weiss, Jr. The statistical graphics are by Melissa S. Meyer. My thanks to all. Errors and reckless inferential leaps remain the responsibility of the author.

I believe that newspapers will survive. The key to survival will not be in any of the techniques described in this book but rather in the attitude that it tries to encourage: an attitude of searching cooperation between managers and researchers as they seek out and solve the researchable questions.

PHILIP MEYER

Chapel Hill, N.C.
January 1984

The Newspaper Survival Book

INTRODUCTION / I

The Rise of the
Marketing Approach / 1.

For some of us, the idea of marketing the news seems a little bit shady. We have our reasons.

A generation ago, when the daily newspaper was the dominant news medium, publishers did not feel very strong economic pressures to offer high-quality editorial products. A reader needed the local newspaper more than the publisher needed any given reader. Even in competitive markets, organizational survival depended more on keeping advertisers happy than on nurturing contented readers. A few publishers, like the Knight brothers of Akron and Miami, could see far enough down the road to realize that reader satisfaction enhances and preserves a paper's worth to advertisers. But, with no strong competition from other kinds of information sources, the connection was not obvious.

In that situation, temptation was strong to run newspapers with short-term satisfaction for advertisers as the uppermost goal. Domineering and unethical business offices were not uncommon. Many newspapermen of my generation have worked in city rooms where copy frequently came across the desk on yellow paper and bearing the slug "BOM," for "business office must." It usually contained a plug for some advertiser, and the yellow paper and the slug were the signal that the copy was to sail through the editing process untouched.

At one such paper, in a Kansas town where I worked as a reporter in the days when TV was still in its infancy, I learned that the local television station had begun broadcasting in color. Awed by this technological advance, I wrote a story about it. The story was killed. The editor's explanation: the business office didn't want people in that town to learn about the availability of color broadcasts until the local retailers had unloaded their existing stock of top-of-the-line black-and-white sets.

Such stories are rare today. Abuses of business office influence have been countered with a standard that holds that business and editorial operations of a newspaper should be as separate as church and state. In some organizations, this meant keeping editors and business managers at

3

arm's length and more. Sometimes they hardly knew each other. The theory underlying this separation was that the two sides operated from conflicting ethical principles, and that the only way to protect the integrity of the paper as a whole was to build the wall of separation.

That view was naive and inaccurate. The two ethical systems are different, but neither is absolute nor are they irreconcilable.

The editorial side operates under a service ethic. Its governing principle is that whatever serves the public, especially the reading public, is good. Editors and reporters should have the freedom to discover and impart the truth about events that affect their readers. It is a sound ethic, and journalists who subscribe to it do so with justifiable pride. However, there are situations where it does not work as smoothly as we might like.

Suppose, for example, that an editor knows what is good for the community but can't get anyone to pay attention to him. Knowledge is worthless if it is not communicated, and it is not possible to communicate effectively to an audience that is unwilling to expend the energy needed to receive the message. All of the twists and turns of the city council as it gropes its way toward resolution of a problem or controversy may seem of vital importance to the editor, but his job does not end with a mere chronicling of those details. The information has to be put in a form that will make the readers want to receive it. In short, information must be made marketable.

The Market Ethic

On the business side, a market ethic traditionally prevails. This ethic is based on the premise that people get what they pay for, and the duty of a business is to provide what they will pay for. Much of the activity in Western civilization is governed by the market ethic, but it is no more absolute than the news side's service ethic. There are situations where the market ethic is simply not adequate. Externally imposed scarcity can provide such a situation. When gasoline was in short supply in the 1970s, it was not generally agreed that whatever was on hand should go to the highest bidders.

In addition, there are certain products of organized society for which it is recognized that the market alone would not provide fair distribution. Education is one. Tradition holds that every person should receive as much as he or she can use. Justice is another. The benefits of civil and criminal justice are supposed to be available to everyone. In practice, a mixed ethic operates, with society trying to set minimum standards for the distribution of these benefits while the marketplace is free to provide enhanced benefits for those who can pay.

Yet another ethical standard has begun to prevail at some newspaper companies, chiefly those that have become part of large corporations. It is the growth ethic, and its principle is that whatever makes a company bigger is good. It can be more than just a refinement of the market ethic and may indeed conflict with it when an organization faces a choice between maximizing profit and maximizing growth. While growth may maximize long-term profitability, the connection is not always a sure one, and some students of American business (Bing, 1980) believe it is not always rational. Growth may be emotionally satisfying to a company's management, and it may make an executive's job seem more important, but it is difficult to rationalize as a public good. Neither editorial nor business sides of news organizations seem to be immune from its influence.

The market ethic, however, does carry an arguable public benefit. Adam Smith's "hidden hand" can lead newspaper management to spend its operating budget on producing information that people will want to receive. An editor should at least approach the market ethic with an open mind and give some tentative consideration to the possibility that there might be some value in it. Quite often the market ethic can be applied in ways that are perfectly compatible with the more traditional service ethic. An editor cannot be very effective in trying to serve a community that does not want to be served, and so, whether he or she is conscious of it or not, the task of the editor is to include some salesmanship in his or her job. This idea is not as radical as it might seem. Every decision about what to put in the paper or what to leave out involves an implied effort to persuade the public of the rightness of that decision. And to persuade is to market. If the readers disagree with the editor to the point that they stop buying the paper, they are no longer susceptible to that editor's persuasion or judgment. It follows that successful marketing is a prerequisite to successful service.

If this limitation on editorial autonomy is difficult to accept, consider the question of ultimate control over what is published. There is always some authority higher than the editor. Different societies and different organizations vest that authority in different ways, but it is always there, and no law of nature gives an editor automatic control over the hearts and minds of his audience.

When that authority is vested in a business organization, the consumer, through the marketplace, holds the ultimate power. Would we really have it any other way? The alternatives are not especially appealing. Government-run newspapers could be free of reader influence, but who would want to read them? Special interest groups sometimes publish information in newspaper-like format, but they seldom gain our confidence as suppliers of information for the general public. Perhaps newspapers should be run by charitable foundations. The *St. Petersburg Times* and the *Houston Chronicle* enjoy that distinction, but even charitable foundations need to operate in the black. Without that discipline, the organization that Nelson Poynter's will created in St. Petersburg would risk losing touch with its readership. Organizations that are not accountable to the people whom they serve tend to become wrapped up in their own narrow concerns.

Newspapers run by private businesses have an advantage over all other forms of ownership and management because the market system makes the owners and managers accountable to the people who use the services. If a newspaper does not adequately serve its readers, they can vote with their feet — or, more precisely, their pocketbooks. They can stop reading and turn their attention to wherever they can find a better bargain. And they do. News people might prefer a system in which the editors could, in their wisdom, decide what was good for readers and then give it to them whether they wanted it or not. But that is not the real world, and the need to elicit that daily vote of confidence cast with the readers' quarters is a healthy and necessary check on newspaper management.

A Challenge for Editors

Given the necessity for editors to live with this constraint, the challenge for the idealistic editor becomes one of packaging and delivering news that he or she believes is important for the community in a way that will make the reader glad to part with that 25 cents. This by definition is a marketing problem.

For some newspapers, acceptance of this fact has meant the abandonment of long-established ways of doing things. For years, the *Baltimore*

Sun was supported by a mass audience while edited for a limited elite. The paper affected what a reporter from the rival *Washington Post* called "a patrician detachment from its home city."

> Local stories rarely played on the front page. The paper was run in the spirit of noblesse oblige by four well-to-do families who shared a belief that they had a duty to provide the leaders of government with reliable information. So the *Sun* looked beyond rough and tumble Baltimore to Washington, where it has kept a large staff for decades, and overseas, where it maintains eleven bureaus, from Cape Town to Tokyo.

If the *Sun* gave its readers what it thought they needed, its editors believed that they needed factual but dull institutional and political stories about the detailed workings of officials and official bodies. It was a paper of record, not a reader-oriented paper. The paper enjoyed an excellent reputation for decades, but by the early 1980s the blue collar workers of Baltimore were voting with their quarters, and their declining support forced a reevaluation of that paper's interesting traditions. "We have to quit worrying about whether we get read in high places," said the new publisher, "and worry about whether we get read in Maryland" (Brown, 1982).

When circulation is falling, it is easier to convince oneself of the importance of marketing. The readership statistics from 1970 to the present have been a powerful spur. The purpose of this book is not to make an unqualified plea for the virtues of marketing, but to caution editors and other newspaper managers to use these techniques carefully and well. The marketing approach, if badly handled, can be every bit as painful and debilitating as a total disregard for the market. Taking a poll to see what the readers want and then giving it to them is not good marketing. The dynamics of the relationship between a newspaper and its readers are much more complicated than that. The intuition of most editors is worth far more than any reader poll. Nevertheless, there are ways to use polls and other quantitative research techniques to reduce the amount of guesswork that goes into editorial decision making. The argument of this book is that an editor can use marketing research to enhance and extend his or her creative power.

Lee Hills of Knight-Ridder Newspapers once said, "When an editor starts thinking that what's good for him and his personal beliefs and prejudices is good for his newspaper, it may be time to change editors."

He was right, but today a problem arises from the other direction. The editor who believes that he can relinquish his judgment to that of the public opinion pollsters and who uses research as a substitute for creative power also ought to be replaced. Market research should be used to reduce risks and strike balances.

That newspapers in general need to try harder to become essential in the lives of their readers is no longer in doubt. Newspaper readership used to be an entrenched habit, and, at least in monopoly situations, even the worst-edited newspapers were consistently and widely read. In the 1950s and 1960s, on an average day, eight American adults out of ten would read a newspaper. Around 1970 that number began falling. One source of tracking data for the newspaper readership picture is the National Opinion Research Center at the University of Chicago. At irregular intervals since 1967, surveys run by the Center have asked this question of a national sample of adults: "How often do you read a daily newspaper—every day, two or three times a week, once a week, less than once a week, or never?"

This chart shows what has happened to the percent who say they read every day:

Every-Day Readers

1967	1972	1975	1977	1978	1982	1983
73%	69%	66%	62%	57%	54%	56%

The reason for this decline in newspaper readership is not difficult to perceive. New information technology has brought into being many competing claims for the reader's time. Measurements of reading time vary, depending on the method, but the most conservative measure comes from time diaries where the respondent accounts for every activity of the day. In 1960, according to a time-use study by John Robinson of the University of Maryland, the average adult in the United States spent 23 minutes with a daily newspaper. By 1970, the newspaper's share of the reader's day had slipped to fourteen minutes. What were people doing with that extra time?

The New Competition

Mostly, they were using other media. Television has been taking an increasing amount of time. New technological developments associated with television, including video games, the multiplicity of channels on cable, direct satellite-to-home broadcasting, and the use of videotex to let the user select printed information to be displayed on the home screen, all promised to provide even more television-related competition for newspaper time.

Technology has also increased the competition from print media. Printing is no longer as labor intensive as it once was, and a great variety of specialized print publications now compete with newspapers for reader time. Shoppers and controlled circulation publications can deliver total market coverage to advertisers as well as traditional central city newspapers can.

Surprisingly, this increased competition has not been a financial disaster for most newspapers. For most newspapers, the business today is more profitable than it has ever been, with business offices compensating for lagging circulation revenue by boosting advertising rates. Advertisers have endured this because they recognize that a major newspaper is still a very efficient way to deliver the message, and they appreciate the quality of newspapers' remaining circulation. Newspaper subscribers tend to be better educated and more affluent—and therefore better customers—than nonreaders.

Advertisers have not been so tolerant, however, when it comes to supporting a newspaper that is clearly second or third in its market. With all of the choices among competing media that an advertiser faces, a newspaper that does not dominate its market is among the least attractive. For this reason, some spectacular newspaper failures have occurred in the face of general prosperity in the newspaper business. The *Washington Star* and the *Philadelphia Bulletin*, both good papers, died because they did not dominate their markets. Advertisers turned to the leading paper first, and, in most instances, considered the second paper unnecessary duplication. This is the hard fact about the newspaper business today. Not even monopoly newspapers can count on dominating their markets. They do face and will face increasing competition from alternative media plus continuing challenges to traditional market boundaries. To maintain their dominance they will have to do more than just sit there and do things the way they've always done them. Every newspaper, no matter how fat and secure it feels at the moment, should reevaluate its standing in the community and its relationship with its readers.

Newspapers sell more than information. They sell influence. In addition to delivering the advertiser's message to the consumer, a newspaper provides a credible and essential medium in which that message can be packaged. A newspaper is a creator and reinforcer of community values, and it can even create a community where none existed before by alerting segments of its readers to their common interests. The more essential it is to that community, the more useful it is to advertisers. We of the editorial side can rejoice in this phenomenon without feeling that we have become mercenaries, because it provides a rationale for editorial quality. Lee Hills and John S. Knight of the Knight-Ridder newspapers recognized this when they were building a newspaper chain from bases in Akron and Miami. "No company ever prospered indefinitely with a mediocre product," said Lee Hills after the company had become the second largest newspaper publisher in the nation. "Whenever the product is mediocre, something else may come along to capture a share of its market or even to replace it outright."

The danger of that "something else" coming along, remote when Knight and Hills were building their organization, is clear and present today. And so it is important for editors to understand the needs that newspapers fulfill and to use the innate strengths of their product to form a needed service so thoroughly and so well that no other competing medium can match it. It can be done. The chart presented earlier in this chapter provides a rather depressing look at the trend in newspaper readership. To convince you that all is not lost, that there is some hope in learning the tricks described in this book, I have saved the good news. The following chart shows what has happened to the number of people who read a newspaper less than once a week. It has hardly varied since the studies first began.

Readers—Less Than Once a Week

1967	1972	1975	1977	1978	1982	1983
9%	9%	10%	11%	13%	12%	12%

The fact that these hard-core nonreaders have not increased their numbers significantly should be very encouraging. The problem editors face is not converting the nonreader to readership. That would be extremely difficult and not very rewarding, particularly when one considers the quality of those nonreaders. They tend to be downscale economically, poorly educated, not very good prospects for the advertiser, and not the sort of people to whom we would enjoy marketing editorial products. The problem instead is one of increasing the frequency of readership among those people who do see a newspaper at least once a week. To hold readership constant or even effect a long-term reversal of the downward trend, it is necessary to convert some regular but less-than-daily readers to more frequent readership. And that is a marketing problem if there ever was one.

The Strategic Environment
for Newspapers / 2.

Things change, observes the protagonist of an otherwise unmemorable newspaper novel of the 1950s. When a change comes that you don't like, you roll with the punch. And, if you do like it, you ride it hell-for-leather, for all it is worth. The study of trends is trendy these days, and there is no shortage of people willing to tell you about the underlying tides of social change that are likely to affect our lives and our enterprises.

Spotting the trends is easy. Deciding how to respond to them is not. In this chapter, we are going to examine one of the most basic, stable, and predictable of all social trends, the changing age structure, and try to assess its impact on the newspaper business. But first, a quick checklist of five current trends having an impact on the new business right now:

Trend No. 1: The Internationalization of Reporting. Modern communication and transportation technologies have made the world more interdependent. Economic problems are no longer localized to a single country or region. Newspaper readers found out about this when the development problems of certain Third World nations translated themselves into gasoline lines in the United States. Transportation and communications technologies have turned the world into a single market-place where the United States no longer competes as effectively in many of its traditional industries. The planet is smaller, and the opportunities for one nation to stick an elbow into the ribs of another, with good intentions or bad, are greatly amplified.

Reader surveys show a high level of interest in foreign news. In part, this may be due to a rational connection made by readers between their own lives and what happens overseas. It may also be in part stimulated by what readers see on television, where live coverage gives foreign news an immediacy it lacked before satellite communications.

The best young foreign correspondents are reacting to this interest by going beyond the traditional coverage of wars, riots, and shifts in power to reporting on comparative cultures and different ways of handling universal human and economic problems. They are becoming more specialized in the ways of the nations they cover, and the old adage that a good reporter is good anywhere—meaning that special knowledge or training is not needed—no longer holds.

Trend No. 2: The Latinization of the United States.   Twenty years ago, 80% of our immigrants came from Europe. Today, 80% come from Spanish-speaking and Asian countries. Immigration accounts for about ⅓ of the population growth in the U.S., and much of it is illegal, from south of the border (Fallows, 1983). By 1981, persons of Spanish origin identified by the census were 6.5% of the U.S. population, and they were not all concentrated in the border states. The largest Hispanic markets in 1983 were Los Angeles, New York, Miami, San Antonio, and Chicago. The population pressures from the South are immense, and this flow is likely to continue. Because theirs is such a vigorous culture, the Latins should have a lasting effect that is even greater than their numbers would suggest. The growth in Spanish publications, Spanish broadcasting stations—and in Miami, a daily Spanish-language section of a major metropolitan newspaper—are signs of media adaptation to this emerging market.

Trend No. 3: The "Compunications" Revolution.   This is a made-up word to cover the merging of information processing and information-transmitting technologies. More and more of our national product involves the collection, processing, and distribution of information. And the tools with which to do it are becoming simultaneously cheaper and more powerful. My first efforts at survey analysis were done with an IBM computer that cost nearly $10 million (in constant 1983 dollars) when it was new. It occupied a very large room at the Harvard Computation Center. As of this writing, the same job can be done on a computer that costs less than $10,000 and sits on a desk top. These quantitative changes are so great as to make a qualitative change in the market for information. An information provider's task may not be so much to find something new for the customer as to help the customer manage the information already available.

Trend No. 4: The Segmentation of Interests.   In the move from an industrial society to one in which information and services are the main products, the economic pressure for uniformity is swiftly eroding. The assembly line and the economies of scale of mass production led to mass marketing. Today, the mass is being broken up, and this break-up is reflected in the kinds of media that are created and sold. Instead of a few messages distributed to the many, we have many messages distributed to the few (Toffler, 1980). Newspapers are much fatter than they were 50 years ago, when a 32-page paper was considered to be near the outer limit of tolerance, not because people are reading more, but because each issue is aimed simultaneously at many different audiences, each of which reads only a piece of the whole.

Trend No. 5: The Changing Age Structure. You should have been born in 1930. Demographers call those of us who entered the world between the start of the Depression and World War II "the Good Times Generation." Ours was a period of low birth rates, meaning that the schools were always big enough to hold us, there was never a teacher shortage while we were being educated, and there was little competition for entry-level jobs when our educations were finished. As we climbed the career ladder, we encountered little competition, because there was always a shortage of people at whatever stage of development we happened to be in at the time.

The Baby Boomers—those born in the postwar period—were in the reverse situation. Life for them has always been tough and competitive. Their schools were crowded, teachers were scarce, good jobs hard to find. This baby boom was greater than any ever recorded, and its effect on the age structure of the population will last until the middle of the next century. The center of the bulge is occupied by those born in 1958 and 1959. Because newspaper readership is related to age, with the daily reading habit most often settling in around age 30, newspaper circulation began to benefit from the baby boom around 1980. That benefit should continue to grow until the end of the decade, by which time the number of people entering the age bracket of maximum reading will begin to decline. Until then, newspaper circulation is getting a boost from a national force of extreme power—an example of a trend to ride for all it is worth. When this generation was entering young adulthood, however, we had a natural force that inhibited newspaper growth because the young people were not particularly interested in what we had to sell and there were so many of them.

Of all these trends, the changing age structure is the easiest to study, because we know exactly what is going to happen. Everyone ages at the same rate, and we can get a good estimate of the number of people who will be 30 years old in ten years by counting the number who are 20 now and making corrections for death plus in- and out-migration. Yet things still catch us by surprise, particularly the way a quantitative difference turns into a qualitative difference. The baby boomers are different in ways other than their numbers. What follows now is an attempt to track their effect on the newspaper business.

The Youth Market

When newspaper readership began its decline at the beginning of the last decade, newspaper managers began adopting modern marketing methods to try to reverse the trend. Much of their effort was directed at the youth market. Young people, because of the population bulge from the postwar baby boom, which peaked in 1958–1959, were particularly salient at that time. Not only their unprecedented numbers gave them visibility, but also their political activity on behalf of civil rights, the counter-culture, and the antiwar movement. When one-shot market surveys showed that younger people were less likely than their elders to read a newspaper on an average day, the intuitive judgment that youth was the source of the problem seemed to be confirmed.

This generation gap in newspaper readership was detected well before the baby boomers came of age. However, the difference did not appear to be very great until the 1960s. A solid sixteen-point gap was found in 1967 when Sidney Verba and Norman Nie measured self-estimates of reading frequency in their landmark study on political participation in America (1972). Earlier data collected by Wilbur Schramm (1946) and Robert Davis (1957) and analyzed by John P. Robinson and Leo W. Jeffres (1979) show that in the days before the saturation of the television market, newspaper readership was uncorrelated or only slightly correlated with age.

A plausible hypothesis to explain this effect is readily available. Television was an attractive substitute for the newspaper in meeting the entertainment needs of the unsophisticated. It was not so successful in meeting more serious information needs. The people who remained the most loyal to newspapers were those who were somewhat settled, had a stake in their community, and a desire to keep up with local public affairs. At what age does a person acquire these characteristics? The Newspaper Advertising Bureau studied children from six to seventeen and found that the process of habit formation begins in the years when reading skills are acquired. By aggregating a large number of cases from the General Social

Survey of the National Opinion Research Center, one can examine readership by very fine age groupings and find the point at which the habit of reading a newspaper every day begins to take hold. In looking at the surveys for the 1970s and the early part of the 1980s and using the smoothing procedures proposed by John Tukey (1977), we can see a threshold at about the age of 30.

The hypothesis assumes a simple, one-time effect. Before television, all age groups read the newspaper more or less equally. Television came and substituted for one limited segment of the newspaper's functions. If that were the end of the story, newspaper managers could relax, secure with the functions they had left, confident that as the younger generation aged, it would adopt the media habits of its elders. As time went on, however, the data did not confirm that comforting belief.

Some Underlying Effects

An age-behavior correlation can be associated with any of three underlying effects or with any combination of the three (Miller and Levitin, 1976). The optimistic assumption of those of us who were worrying about newspaper readership in the late 1960s and early 1970s was that a *life-cycle* phenomenon was at work. Young people were slow to adopt the newspaper habit because of competing attractions based on their position in the life cycle, and, as they aged, they would become like the rest of us. Because the young people in question were members of the postwar baby boom generation, a huge expansion of the market was just around the corner.

A second possibility was that we were seeing a *generation* effect. The people who are born during a particular time period may share certain experiences during their formative years that make them forever different from everybody else. If this were the case, the newspaper business would be saddled with a generation—and an oversized generation at that—of permanently low readership.

The third possibility is that *historical* events can affect everyone alive at a certain time, regardless of age, and it can mask as a life cycle or generation effect when the affected population ages and is replaced by people not so affected. Or it can offset or blur coexisting life-cycle and generation effects. What began as a seemingly simple observation—that young people are reading less—suddenly becomes extremely complicated.

What we need here is a straightforward theory to explain the various observations of newspaper readership among age groups for the past two decades. But first we should look at the data. For no very good reason, except that marketing researchers have always done it that way, readership surveys normally look at 18–24 and 25–34 age breaks that unfortunately obscure the threshold effect at 30. Fortunately, there is a publicly archived data set with seven observations from 1967 to 1983 that measures both newspaper readership and exact age, so an analyst can set the age-cutting points anywhere he or she wants. The General Social Survey of the National Opinion Research Center, University of Chicago, asked the question in 1972, 1975, 1977, 1978, 1982, and 1983. In addition, NORC ran the Verba-Nie participation study, which asked the same question with similar methods in 1967. Here is the question: "How often do you read the newspaper—every day, a few times a week, once a week, less than once a week, or never?"

The question is less precise than the industry's standard measurement of "yesterday" readership, but it does have the advantage of having been asked of comparable samples each year.

How Age Groups Have Performed

Here is how different age groups have performed since 1967. The cutting points are set to keep the 18-to-30-year-olds together, and the other cuts are at equal 13-year intervals. The numbers given are the percent who reported reading "every day," and the age categories show age at the time of the interview.

One does not have to stare at this chart very long to see that it looks like, at least through 1982, a diffusion phenomenon. There is loss in all of the age groups, but it comes progressively later with advancing age groups. For the youngest group, the biggest drop arrives in 1972. The phenomenon strikes the next oldest group in the 1975–1977 period. Persons aged 44–56 are untouched by all of this until their readership takes a dive in 1978. And for those 57–69, it doesn't happen until 1982. By then, the impact is totally diffused through the age groupings, and readership among those 31–69 is poised for its rebound in 1983. You will note that these changes are not explained by a generation effect. The upward movement through the age brackets is much too fast to be explained by the aging of a low-readership cohort. How did all this happen?

Every-Day Readers

Age	1967	1972	1975	1977	1978	1982	1983	Loss, 67–83
18–30	61%	49%	51%	42%	38%	38%	35%	26%
31–43	77	75	68	60	53	48	52	25
44–56	78	79	73	74	66	64	73	5
57–69	77	77	75	78	77	66	73	4
70+	75	71	76	69	73	70	69	6
TOTAL	73	69	66	62	57	54	56	17

Diffusion theory has its roots in rural sociology. It began after agricultural colleges noticed that farmers were not seizing upon their inventions of hybrid grains, pesticides, and other technological innovations with immediate and grateful joy. And so they began to inquire into the process by which innovation is passed along. The topic is also of interest to diplomats trying to help developing countries join the modern world through transfer of technology and to marketers seeking to overcome consumer resistance to the new and unfamiliar. What they have generally found out (Rogers and Shoemaker, 1971) is that the rate of adoption of an innovation follows the normal, bell-shaped curve. It proceeds slowly at first, accelerates, and levels off when about half the eventual adopters have made the move. From that point forward, adoption proceeds at a decreasing rate.

Marketers classify the people at the beginning tail of the diffusion curve, the first 2 or 3%, as "innovators." These are venturesome folks who seek "the hazardous, the rash, the daring and the risky," according to Rogers and Shoemaker, but they are not necessarily opinion leaders or role models for the rest of the market. The key people for marketers are the next wave, the adopters on the accelerating part of the curve, the 10 to 15% whom the marketers call "early adopters." These people tend to be more integrated into the social system than the innovators; they have leadership roles, and the great mass of the market will tend to follow them.

Early Adoption and Age

What makes all of this relevant to the case at hand is that sometimes, although by no means always, there is a correlation between time of adoption and age, with younger people adopting first. Rogers and

Shoemaker found cases with and without this correlation. But the fact that it exists at all can at least give us the courage to speculate that the upward creep of readership loss through the age brackets is really a case of negative diffusion. When diffusion is negative, the behavior spreading through the population is not adoption but its reverse—in this case, the ending of the newspaper habit.

There is anecdotal evidence to support a belief that, when income is held constant, new information-processing technology is adopted more readily by young people. Look at the young, self-made millionaires in the computer business. In occupations where computers have been introduced for the first time, the younger people have generally made the transition more eagerly—as anyone who was in a newsroom when computer terminals replaced typewriters will remember. And entrepreneurs in the many versions of videotex now on or heading toward the market are targeting their early efforts toward younger consumers.

Television is the oldest and most dramatic mass communications innovation of our time, and its fascination for youth was instantly apparent. But there have been other, more subtle innovations, including the proliferation of highly specialized print media. The underlying effect of new technology has been to make increased specialization of mass communications economically desirable (Maisel, 1973). Because the resources available for consuming information are limited (McCombs, 1972), the new media tend to squeeze out the old. The squeeze takes place first among those who adapt to the new media the most easily and whose habits of using the old have had a shorter period of reinforcement—in short, the young.

Viewed as an age-related phenomenon, what has happened is a combination of historical event and life-cycle effect. The historical event is the explosion and fragmentation of mass media, and, while it happened to everyone at the same time, persons in the earlier stages of the life cycle were the most vulnerable to its effects. They were the early adopters, and the rest of the population followed, in general order of age.

A theory should have an equation to go with it. One can be derived simply by charting the relationship between age and readership loss. Figure 1 charts the midpoint of each age bracket on the Y axis while X represents time in years. The data points show the year in which each age bracket first showed a daily readership loss of at least ten points. We are handicapped here by the fact that NORC made no readership meas-

FIGURE 1

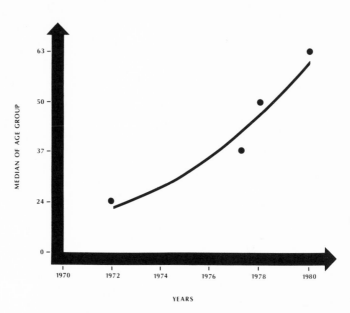

Make that assumption, and Figure 1 yields a smooth curve with an accelerating rate of diffusion. The equation that describes it is $\text{Log}Y = .052X - 101$, and it explains 96% of the variance. Of course, explaining a lot of variances is no big feat with so few data points, especially where one is imputed to fit the theory. But the exercise does confirm the symmetry of what is seen by studying the table with the naked eye.

urement between 1978 and 1982, a crucial period because other data, chiefly that of the Simmons Market Research Bureau, suggests that readership bottomed out about 1980. Had such a measure been taken, it probably would have shown that the last group to feel the loss, ages 57–69, took that loss in 1980.

Make that assumption, and Figure 1 yields a smooth curve with an accelerating rate of diffusion. The equation that describes it is $\text{Log}Y = .052X - 101$, and it explains 96% of the variance. Of course, explaining a lot of variances is no big feat with so few data points, especially where one is imputed to fit the theory. But the exercise does confirm the symmetry of what is seen by studying the table with the naked eye.

A Look at the Cohorts

Now, how about the upturn in newspaper readership in 1983? The theory of negative diffusion doesn't quite predict it, but it does suggest that once the effect has spread to all age groups, it doesn't have any place else to go, and the worst may be over. For a clearer picture, we need to look at age cohorts. In the following table, respondents are divided according to the period in which they were born rather than the age at the time of the interview. In this way, we can see clearly the resultant of life cycle, historical, and generation effects, because a cohort represents a constant population. Here the divisions are set to match easily recognizable historical periods: the baby boomers, the Depression and World War II babies, the post-World War I generation, and those people born from the turn of the century to World War I.

The baby boomers, it turns out, have been remarkably stable. While they do not increase in readership as they progress through the life cycle, they are not regressing either. The older generations, viewed through 1982, show a pattern that is at least consistent with the notion that once the readership loss is felt in a cohort, it does not accelerate, and the readership level tends toward stability. Therefore, by 1982, the negative diffusion effect had run its course and newspapers could look forward to a period of stability. But this still does not explain the vigor of the rebound among the middle cohorts in 1983. Have they simply grown weary of other media and are drifting back to newspapers? Have the industry's marketing effects finally made themselves felt? Or is the movement merely regression toward the mean?

To find out, it may be necessary for future scholars to extend the above tables through the end of the century. Another wave of technological innovation in mass communications approaches even now, and it appears to be at least as youth-biased as the wave that is now spent. If videotex and teletext show even some of the promise that their creators envision, the newspaper industry may once again cope with the phenomenon of negative diffusion as the effects of change sweep upward through the age groupings.

When we consider that this almost overpowering effect comes from just one of many different kinds of social change, it is easy to become a little

Every-Day Readers

Year Born	1967	1972	1975	1977	1978	1982	1983
1945–54	—	47%	53%	45%	43%	50%	48%
1930–44	69	69	68	61	61	56	66
1918–29	78	79	75	77	68	66	78
1900–17	77	75	76	79	76	70	68

discouraged. That is not the intended effect of this chapter nor of this book. Following social trends is important for planning purposes and giving context to research goals, but we should not abdicate our planning to the people who chart such trends. James K. Batten (1983), president of Knight-Ridder Newspapers, put it this way to a meeting of publishers: "If we give too much weight to those underlying trends that supposedly are pulling society inexorably in this or that direction, we risk underestimating our ability to decide what we want the future to be, and then to make it happen."

Or, as Seymour Martin Lipset, the political scientist, put it some years earlier:

> Let us not be paralyzed by numbers that do not give us the sum we would like to see. We can continue to change the equation. The future can be what we make of it. . . .

The Limits of Conventional
Newspaper Research   3.

Editors who use market research for the first time find the result some-times disappointing. Perhaps they expect too much. Perhaps the sup-pliers of commercial news research oversell their wares.

In any event, news research—defined as marketing research applied to circulation-building and improvement of the newspaper—is no longer viewed as a panacea for circulation problems, if indeed it ever was.

Success stories can be found, but editors too often complain that usable research findings are mere restatements of common sense. When some-thing new and surprising is found, an editor may still be left without a clue as to what to do about it.

The problem may be that using marketing methods in the news busi-ness is much more difficult than research-oriented news people believed when they first began to climb aboard the marketing bandwagon in the 1970s (Burroughs, 1981). This move was made in response to the relative decline in newspaper readership discovered in the early 1970s. It was also stimulated in part by increased interest in advertising research, which in turn had been inspired by a Newspaper Advertising Bureau program for coordinated audience research. Newspapers were making large outlays to develop audience measurements to use as sales tools for the advertising department, and they began including newsrooms in their planning.

By the middle 1970s, large-scale survey research projects dedicated to measuring reader attitudes toward the editorial product became com-mon. But by the 1980s, such studies had lost their novelty. Marketing research became routinized, and it was no longer looked to for new and surprising revelations. Managers began to realize that marketing tech-niques perfected for packaged goods such as toothpaste or laundry deter-gent could not be easily or automatically transferred to newspapers (Hirt, 1983). Projects became targeted less often to the editorial product and were more likely to be designed to serve all departments of the news-paper. There was one advantage to the routinization process, however. Key question items were more likely to become benchmarks for repeated measurement so that a newspaper could receive early warnings of any important changes in its readers' outlooks.

Such an outcome is not unusual when research is applied to decision making. Government policy makers went through a similar cycle in the 1960s. Computers made powerful analytic techniques available for the first time, and there was a general feeling of euphoria as the tools of social science were applied to public policy questions on a scale never before attempted. In 1966, Robert E. Lane wrote an article for the *American Journal of Sociology* titled "The Decline of Politics and Idelogy in a Knowledgeable Society." In it, he argued that "the domain of politics" was yielding to "the domain of knowledge." As learned investigators became more influential, public policy decisions would be made "with rationality and efficiency."

Granted that things like rationality and efficiency in public policy are difficult to measure, one would be hard-pressed to demonstrate that there was very much more of either two decades later. What happened was that the politicians, who have the difficult responsibility of balancing competing interests and finding a workable consensus, were not freed at all of those responsibilities by "the domain of knowledge." For one thing, the knowledge produced by the social scientists assigned to policy work was not all that clear much of the time. And even when it was clear, acting on it still required a political process that was often irrational and inefficient.

A Problem of Communication

Moreover, as some people at the front line of those battles have pointed out (Greenberger, Crenson, and Crissey, 1976), there is a problem of communication. Researchers and decision makers come from different subcultures, and they have different constraints and different interests. They work at different tempos. The policymaker has a short time horizon, the researcher a long one. Getting them to mesh is not an easy task.

Exactly these same sorts of problems have afflicted the relationship between newspaper editors and newspaper researchers. An editor's decisions involve a great many variables, more than the researcher can quantify or even know about. The researcher focuses on a narrow and quantifiable problem that may be moot by the time an answer is obtained. Editors need to know so many things that they have trouble sorting out the information needs that are researchable from those that are not.

Because they are not trained in research, they cannot do this sorting process by themselves. The researcher, lacking the editor's real-world experience, may not be of much help.

As a result, imaginative applications of research are distressingly rare. Researchers tend to sell techniques that are easy to understand, such as simple counts of readers with different characteristics. The limit of sophistication is often simple cross-tabulation.

Cross-tabulation is making comparison of characteristics across different groups. For example, knowing that 56% of adults read the newspaper on an average day may not be as interesting as knowing that 60% of the women but only 50% of the men read it.

Wringing More Out

Academic researchers who see commercial research reports are struck by the tendency of newspapers to fund expensive studies and then settle for computer-generated cross-tabulations displaying only superficial relationships. The academics are used to wringing more out.

This problem is not peculiar to newspaper research. The National Research Council recently commissioned a panel of distinguished social scientists to review "survey measurement of subjective phenomena." Its report, issued in 1981, notes that:

> It is well known to investigators with a major commitment to survey research that most of the data collected are never examined in a searching way. The ratio of analysis to collection is too low, and this is particularly distressing because analysis is relatively inexpensive compared with the costs of data collecting.

The panel sees an economic reason for this misallocation of resources. Survey research is a labor-intensive business generating a large cash flow. An organization created to do this research comes to depend on that cash flow and therefore concentrates on bringing in business to generate new data instead of taking the time to wring everything out of the old.

The most successful suppliers of newspaper research have been those recognizing the efficiency to be gained in standardizing both data collection methods and reports, so that results can easily be fitted into a prepackaged format.

Simple cross-tabulation lends itself nicely to this kind of packaging. But

editors who compare studies across markets have noticed this standardi-
zation and decried what they call the "cookie cutter" approach. An editor
knows that his market is unique and suspects that overstandardization in
research reporting may obscure the important nuances in the attitudes of
his or her audience.

There is a simple and low-cost solution to this problem, and that is to do
more secondary analysis.

A secondary analyst is someone who takes an unhurried, second look at
the original researcher's data, running it through the computer again,
trying new ways of defining variables, introducing controls, changing
cutting points, and looking at things the original researcher may not have
thought about or had time to check.

Some of the larger newspaper organizations maintain an in-house capacity for secondary analysis. It is not uncommon for them to produce
internal reports that suggest modification of the original researcher's con-
clusions or even to disagree with them altogether. The problem with
secondary analysis is that it takes time. Managers already impatient with
the pace of the research process are not likely to countenance many
leisurely ruminations over the data. However, when a new problem
comes up, one for which the data were not intended but to which they
nevertheless apply, secondary analysis can save time as well as bring a
new viewpoint to bear.

Fresh and critical viewpoints are needed. A few researchers, such as
John Mauro of Media General, do take the time and effort to try innovative approaches. And Maxwell McCombs, himself an innovator, spotted
some departures from traditional demographic cross-tabs in the flow of
reports through the American Newspaper Publishers Association News
Research Center at Syracuse University. Some researchers are beginning
to use political or psychological approaches to explain readership, and
these can be more stimulating to an editor's thinking than the traditional
demographics.

The Need for Theoretical Models

One problem with the early applications of news research may be that
editors expected to get straightforward answers to questions that were not
straightforward at all. An editor eager for a demographic analysis would

have no clear idea of what he or she wanted to find out, and the mandate to the researcher would be, "Tell me all about the readers." Disillusionment would set in when the stack of eye-numbing computer tables showing readership by demographics did indeed tell all about the readers and yet not tell what to do. The fault can be the editor's if he or she approaches the task of defining the research without a clear notion of the process by which newspapers and readers interact.

The editor has, in social science jargon, no "theoretical model," no structure to guide in the assembling and studying of data. Without such a model, one is reduced to browsing among the numbers without knowing what to look for or what to do if it is found.

An editor who once considered dropping "Dick Tracy" from the comic page is an illustration of this problem. "Tell me," he implored the research department, "How many of the readers read 'Dick Tracy'?"

A month later, the research department came back with the answer: 23 percent.

"Thank you," the editor is said to have replied. "By the way, is 23 percent a large number or a small number?"

Because no one can think clearly about a complicated problem without some kind of model, editors have taken to forming models unconsciously, like folklore. The most common is something that might be called the "referendum model." If lots of people are interested in a subject, then news about that subject should appear in the newspaper.

Carried to an extreme, this could result in what the late *New York Times* Associate Editor Lester Markel decried as "Gallup editing." And it would not be a very good fit to the realities of today's marketing problems for newspapers.

Some of the folklore models are contradictory. Newspaper executives like models that can be expressed in aphorisms. I knew one who kept saying, "Play to your strengths!" If a survey showed that well-educated people like the newspaper more than less-educated readers, he would urge more highbrow content. But he had another aphorism, always expressed with the same enthusiasm, and it was "Seize your opportunities!" When the same survey showed that young people liked the newspaper less than older people, he would urge shifting the content toward the interests of the younger audience. The two models are, of course, contradictory, and nothing in the computer tabulations ever tells the editor which model to follow. The computer is very good at displaying differences among subgroups, which is what cross-tabulations do. It is not so good at telling what to do about those differences.

The Segmentation Model

Wiser editors adopt some sort of segmentation model. Using the analogy of the cafeteria line, they realize that not every customer going through the line will consume everything offered. Each customer designs a unique menu, and the marketing problem is to provide the choices that will satisfy the largest number of potential customers from a very diverse population. Demographic tables can be of some help in applying the segmentation model, but more powerful tools, such as factor analysis, which can help locate and define clusters of customers and potential customers, are available.

Factor analysis is a way of reducing a large and complicated set of variables by finding a smaller number of underlying factors that have the same explanatory powers but are easier to use. It's done with a computer that looks at the extent to which each variable is correlated with every other variable and then sifts out those groups of variables that tend to be predictors of one another.

Other kinds of models are beginning to emerge. Robin F. Cobbey and Maxwell E. McCombs (1979) have shown researchers how to set priorities for newspaper content. They advocate looking at each feature's referendum score plus one other attribute: the degree to which readership of each feature is grouped with the readership of other features. If "Dick Tracy" is read by people who also read "Steve Canyon," "Spider-Man," and "Mary Worth," then it is safer to drop "Dick Tracy" than if the strip is read by people who read that and nothing else.

Another model, to be covered in Chapter 4, takes the occasional readers into account by considering the association between newspaper readership and interest in a particular topic.

If people who are interested in the topic are more likely to be newspaper readers, the paper is probably already doing a good job of appealing to that interest. But if there is a strong interest in the community that is not associated with newspaper reading, it may signal an opportunity for the newspaper to extend its appeal.

Psychographic studies follow the segmentation model by dividing

readers according to their psychological attributes, as opposed to demographic characteristics, such as sex and age. Because psychographics provide more vivid descriptions, they can help an editor get a clearer picture
of his or her newspaper's readers and the newspaper's position with respect to its competition. In one version of this approach, to be discussed
in detail in Chapter 7, a newspaper audience is divided into several
simple categories according to positions on some attitude scales that measure interesting psychological dispositions.

These scales can be plotted so that an editor can see where a typical
reader of a newspaper appears on the psychological map, where the
typical user of an opposition medium appears, and—just as interest-
ingly—where the inquiring editor appears. That's the good news. The
bad news is that the results can be disappointingly unstable. When you go
back five years or so later, you may find that the psychological profile fits a
different demographic group—or even no one at all—so that what you
had hoped to hold constant has shifted so much that the second measurement is meaningless. Even worse, the clustering techniques are so
powerful that they will produce an appearance of meaning and pattern
where none exists, and it is difficult to distinguish real-world change over
time from random sampling variation.

The Placebo Effect

One of the maddening things about any kind of policy research is that
the hunger for knowledge is often so great that the imputation of meaning
to random patterns can actually be helpful. Primitive societies had specialists who studied the patterns in cracked animal bones or entrails to
determine in which direction to send the hunting party. They were the
first market researchers, and they probably did more good than harm.
They at least randomized the direction of the hunt, which kept the prey
from perceiving the pattern of the search and taking action to keep out of
the way.

Research is useful on a number of levels; one of the most important
uses may be that it stimulates newspaper management to try imaginative
and risky policies that it would not have attempted in the absence of the
research. To describe researchers as "newspaper doctors" becomes less
silly than it sounds if this placebo effect is taken into account. Medical
doctors have long known that about two-thirds of the people they see will

get better no matter what they do. All these patients need from their doctor is some reassurance, some concern, a chance to talk things over, and perhaps a placebo to get them thinking positively again. Newspaper editors can need placebos as much as anyone else.

If editors find the idea of researcher-as-therapist offensive, there is some hope for the most hard-nosed among them at the other end of the spectrum. Sometimes the most satisfying applications of research occur when newspaper management has clear alternative policies in mind and uses research tools to reduce the risk in choosing between those alternatives. The task given the researcher is a formidable one: to predict the future outcome of a proposed policy move and set quantified standards for action.

Action Standards

Difficult as that may sound, such an assignment has the advantage of being clear and specific. Everyone can agree on what they are attempting to measure, and the action standards are clear enough to set in advance of the research.

One of the best examples is a study of newspaper reading habits among Latin Americans in the Miami area, undertaken on behalf of *The Miami Herald* when it was deciding whether to launch a Spanish-language section. A survey by an outside research supplier put the question to the proposed customers in a straightforward manner and yielded a broad and carefully hedged prediction. As an additional check, an in-house, secondary analysis was performed using some indirect measurements and some assumptions about the effects on readership of family composition and length of time the prospective readers had lived in this country.

The latter study produced a more specific prediction. Management decided that the numbers were encouraging enough to justify going ahead, and the Spanish section now accounts for new readership to a degree that has exceeded the researchers' predictions. Also in this category are the current attempts of a number of newspaper companies, including Knight-Ridder, The Times Mirror Company, and Dow Jones and Company Incorporated, to predict the willingness of customers to pay money for electronic delivery of news and information. Their answers, when they come—and if they are right—may well prove to be the most valuable contribution of newspaper research in this century.

Many newspaper researchers employ the concept of action standards to reduce the communications gap between themselves and their editors. An action standard can be simply a number that marks the decision criteria between one policy path and another. If the editor who asked for the "Dick Tracy" survey had used an action standard, he would have decided in advance of the survey what the level of readership would have to be to trigger a decision to drop the comic. And if he could not decide in advance, he could save himself the cost of the survey because he would know that the number, whatever it turned out to be, would not help him. Knight-Ridder had such an action standard in its first videotex trial. It was one number, representing the proportion of trial users who would express interest in paying money for the system. It was fixed in advance of the trial, and the design of the research was centered on obtaining a number to compare to that standard.

You can push this concept too far, of course, and some researchers do. I have known some who consider it a sign of moral weakness or inconsistency to fail to follow the action indicated by the standard once it is established and the research completed. However, the editor or other decision maker has more information than the researcher by the time the research result is obtained. The number the researcher gives him is only one factor in the decision, and the responsible decision maker will not give it more than its proper weight. The purpose of the action standard is not to bind the decision maker to some future course but to ensure that the project is being logically and thoughtfully designed and will produce a result that will help in decision making. It is a way of keeping the research process organized and nothing more.

Some Examples of Innovation

There is also innovative research being done for newspapers by outside suppliers. Tom Holbein and his colleagues at Belden Associates have begun developing and analyzing personal time budgets following a technique developed earlier by Professor John Robinson of the University of Maryland. Consumers keep diaries that show how they spend their time, and this tells something about their lifestyles that can help newspaper managers set their targets, according to Holbein.

Another product of segmentation theory is geographic zoning, and Ruth Clark has applied cluster-analysis techniques to helping editors decide how to define the zones. Looking at a map isn't enough, she says: "We had one client who tried to do it by looking at the map, and if you put the Montagues and the Capulets in the same zone, you couldn't have done a worse job."

This application starts with a survey that asks readers where they shop and what their interests are, particularly as those interests are related to geography. It then uses the computer to search for the geographic alignments that will put like-minded readers together.

Because survey research is the big-ticket, high-cash-flow item in the research arsenal, it tends to get the most attention and the biggest push from suppliers. Other kinds of research, however, can often do a better job because they deal with more stable phenomena than subjective attitudes. Census data provide perhaps the best example. A number of newspapers have used census data for small geographic areas to experiment with regression models to set circulation targets.

To visualize how this works, imagine a map of your city with the census tracts clearly outlined and a number representing circulation penetration (circulation as a percentage of households) clearly marked in each tract. As you view such a map you might say to yourself that one area has above-average penetration, but that's to be expected because it is affluent and suburban, while another neighborhood has low penetration, and that is also to be expected because it is poor and on the rural fringe.

Regression analysis can tell you how much these characteristics should affect a given neighborhood so that you can allow for them with more than educated guesses. It produces an equation that estimates how much circulation goes up with each 1% increase in persons in a given age bracket and how it changes with each 1% change in persons in a given income bracket. With such an equation, you can tell how much penetration to expect in each census tract and compare that expectation with what you actually have.

The result is a better map, one that shows whether a given census tract has more or less than the expected penetration. Where it is less, you can go there and sell newspapers; where it is more, you can go there and find out why in the hope of replicating that experience elsewhere. This can be a tool for editors as well as circulation managers, because it can highlight the fringe areas where circulation is not meeting its potential and can suggest strategies for placing bureaus or otherwise expanding suburban coverage. It is discussed in detail in Chapter 5.

In another departure from survey research, some newspapers are trying to field experiments to see how page-one content affects street sales. In its simplest version, this technique calls for two versions of a front page to be produced, with one version in some racks and another version in others. The difference might be a color photo on page one, as opposed to black and white. What these studies generally show is that newspaper buying is so much a matter of habit that the format or appearance of page one does not make much difference, although content sometimes does.

In a very ambitious version of this experiment, to be described in detail in Chapter 5, *The Philadelphia Inquirer* recorded page-one content and street sales data for a year along with other variables that might affect street sales, including weather, sports events, and whether bus drivers were striking on a particular day. Snow was found to decrease street sales by .1% for each inch of fallen snow, while a transit strike cut street sales by 6%. Lead stories about national or international events pulled slightly better than state or local stories,

Much work remains to be done in this area, but it is conceivable that it could lead to a system for predicting how large the press run should be on a given day, and even the number of newspapers that should be left in a given rack.

Looking Ahead

Where should newspaper research go from here?

It seems clear that more basic research needs to be done. The Newspaper Readership Project, under the leadership of the Newspaper Advertising Bureau, made an enormous contribution during its six years of activity from 1977 to 1983. It produced a body of data that clarifies the relationship between the newspaper and its reader and isolates some of the cause-effect relationships in circulation patterns and reader behavior. Most of the Bureau's studies, including some conducted before the readership project, have been summarized in a handy volume by Leo Bogart (1981). A way should be found to institutionalize that activity and keep it going through good times and bad.

More analysis of existing research is needed. The ANPA News Research Center at Syracuse did an impressive job of collecting proprietary research data from member newspapers, reanalyzing it and developing comparisons across markets and newspaper types. This kind of activity adds an important ingredient to newspaper research because it helps to make the efforts cumulative. More effort in this area is needed, especially when it comes to sharing mistakes. The director of a successful project is happy to share the results. Failures tend to be buried, even though sharing the results of failed projects can contribute as much to learning what works as sharing the successes.

There should be more studies that track readership over time. Such studies are rare because they are costly and require patience. But they can be extremely useful for sorting out murky cause-effect relationships. Chapter 6 will have some specific advice on this subject.

Finally, and perhaps most importantly, newspaper readership needs the development of more explicit models to guide the thinking of researchers and decision makers and to bring them into better synchronization. The next chapter is about making the simple and informal models of everyday research more formal and explicit.

METHODS / II

Models and Their Uses / 4.

We all use models in our thinking about the real world. The models may be highly formal, taking the form of complex equations that can be readily digested only by a computer. Or they may be simple mental models describing the most elementary relationships, such as "Women don't read the sports pages." Simple mental models have the virtue of flexibility. They facilitate thinking, guide the imagination and can be readily adapted to changing circumstances. Their disadvantage is that their use is largely implicit and often unconscious, so they are not readily subject to examination or criticism (Greenberger, 1976).

When survey research is used to guide editorial decison making, the models used are generally of the informal, implicit type. Formal models may be more elegant and precise, but they are not easily focused on the exact question an editor may have to answer: which comic strip to drop; whether to run complete stock tables; how much relative space to allocate to high school and professional sports. A formal model needs an underlying theory to define it. In newspaper research, there are few formal, validated theories to shed light on the relationship between content and readership, between what an editor decides to do and the response of the readers in building the readership habit.

This chapter will introduce you to a model, one not unbearably formal, but that nevertheless helps clarify the thinking that goes into a content decision. Its purpose is to find some pragmatic middle ground between the most formal (and likely unintelligible) models and the everyday mental models that most of us use. By identifying these everyday models and making them explicit, we can overcome the chief disadvantage of their informality: their immunity, because of their low visibility, from examination and criticism.

For illustration, we shall use data from surveys of four medium-sized Knight-Ridder markets in the Southeast. The data were collected by Belden Associates of Dallas in 1975, using the modified probability techniques that are fairly standard in the industry. Neighborhoods with a high

TABLE 1

Four Markets Combined

Percentage "Very Interested"

World Events	58%
National Politics	55
Consumer Information	54
Stretching the Budget	48
Local Issues and Politics	47
Crime and Big Cities	47
The Governor and State	46
Stories about Food	42
Local School Board	38
College Sports	37
Rearing Children	36
Home Decoration	36
Professional Sports	34
Gardening	33
Where to Go in Free Time	32
Household Repairs	32
How to Cope with Modern Life	29
High School Sports	26
Travel	24

proportion of young adults were oversampled to provide an adequate representation for separate analysis of a target group, persons age 25 to 29, and the four samples were pooled to further increase the subsample of that age group. The total sample of 2,950 included 1,128 persons in the 25–29 age range.

Every editor wants to know what subjects the people in the circulation area are most interested in. Respondents in each of the markets were therefore shown a card with a list of topics commonly written about in newspapers and asked, "For each one, please tell me if you are very much interested, somewhat interested, or not at all interested." The topics and the percentage who responded "very interested" to each are shown in Table 1.

The Referendum Model

The display in Table 1 provides all of the numbers needed for the model most frequently applied in editorial research. The editor reads the survey as if it were a referendum to provide a popular check against his or her own tastes and intuitions. If the topics given the most space are also the topics that are the most popular, the editor's judgment is affirmed. If topics given only minimal space prove to be surprisingly popular, then the editor may feel a need to reexamine his or her judgments.

The model is rarely formalized beyond this simple visceral evaluation. However, opportunities for increasing its formality are available, and sometimes they are employed. For example:

1. The rank-order comparison. Before the survey, the editor ranks the subjects according to his estimate of their importance. He may ask his staff to do the same to produce a consensual rank ordering. This order is then compared to the survey ranking to highlight differences between editorial values and popular values. The comparison often produces some surprises.

2. Proportional representation. The number of "very interested" responses in Table 1 can be totaled and used as the base for percentaging each topic's "very interested" response against the total of such responses. This procedure produces a nice list of percentages that add to 100 and can be compared to the percentage of the total news hole actually devoted to each topic. The implicit model assumes that topics ought to be given space in proportion to the total reader interest in them.

3. The plurality test. Sometimes an editor is forced to choose between two topics or features competing for the same space. Under the plurality test, he would simply look at Table 1 and choose whichever topic had the greater popularity.

The referendum model is widely, if unconsciously, applied, although its flaws should be obvious. This review will help to drive home the point that something is to be gained by adding just enough formality to the mental models that they can be examined and criticized.

The flaws of the referendum model are as follows:

1. The model takes inadequate account of intensity. In a referendum, each person gets one vote, whether he or she feels strongly about the question or is indifferent. The editor who blindly follows the model risks being guided by thinly held opinions of little or no consequence at the expense of ignoring less-frequent opinions that are strong enough to have a more important effect on readership.

2. The model does not distinguish between people who have been identified as members of target groups to cultivate and convert to

long-term readership and those whose readership is either assured or unattainable.

3. No consideration is given to duplication of interests. An interest that is uniquely held by a small group may be worth more in net readership than one that touches more people but overlaps with other interests. Readership can often be built by patching many such specialized segments together, but the referendum model tends to guide the editor to the broader and more redundant interests.

Once you become aware that you are in fact using the referendum model, overcoming its flaws is surprisingly easy. Scales can be expanded and distributions examined to identify high-intensity features. Target groups can be analyzed separately. And a couple of tricks based on something called the general linear model (to be explained in Chapter 5) suddenly become handy. One is use of a correlation matrix for a quick eyeball check for interests of high and low duplication. Another is factor analysis to treat the audience as a collection of manageable segments instead of a monolithic whole.

The Target Group Model

Much proprietary research in recent years has focused on target groups. While it represents a gain in sophistication, the model is often nothing more than an application of the referendum model to a specific group. For example, the industry-wide concern in the 1970s over the lower readership rate of young readers led to the singling out of young people as a target group. "Young" has usually been defined as the age range from 18 to 24, mainly because it is a standard census report categorization also used in advertising research.

The implicit theory underlying the target group model is that if members of a target group like a topic better than nonmembers of the group, a newspaper can gain by shifting its emphasis toward that topic just enough to gain new readers more than it will lose old readers. How much is that? We're not ready to address that question just yet.

A wide variety of demographic, psychographic, or other groups can and have been identified as possible targets. In one of the more straightforward applications of this model, the irregular or off-and-on reader is identified as the target, regardless of demographic or psychographic persuasion. Because the normally static figures of newspaper penetration often hide a very high rate of reader turnover, an editor can profitably seek to increase the attention span of the off-and-on readers by appealing to their particular tastes.

A presentation of data for the target-group model is illustrated in Table 2. This table presents the means of a 3-point scale in which "very interested" is worth 3 points and "not at all interested" counts as 1 point, thus using more information than the simple percentages of Table 1. The rank ordering of the young target group is compared with that of older readers so an editor can look for points of difference to stress in the pursuit of the younger reader. The age range of 25-29 was chosen as the target because of evidence in a variety of surveys, both proprietary and published, that the tipping point for acquisition of the newspaper habit comes around the

TABLE 2

Four Markets Combined

	Young		Old	
	Mean	*Rank*	*Mean*	*Rank*
World Events	2.53	1	2.47	1
National Politics and News out of Washington	2.41	2	2.41	2
How to Shop, Consumer Protection, Product Information	2.39	3	2.37	4
Crime and What's Happening in Big Cities	2.29	4	2.31	6
Local Issues and Politics	2.22	5	2.29	7
The Governor and What's Happening in the State Capitol	2.18	6	2.37	3
Stretching the Budget	2.15	7	2.34	5
Stories about Food	2.13	8	2.20	9
Where to Go and What to do in Free Time	2.13	9	1.94	16
College Sports	2.05	10	1.98	13
Rearing Children	2.04	11	1.96	15
Professional Sports	2.03	12	1.91	17
Home Decoration and Furniture	1.94	13	2.15	10
Local School Board Actions	1.91	14	2.20	8
How to Better Cope with Modern Life	1.91	15	1.97	14
Household Repairs	1.86	16	2.10	12
Gardening	1.83	17	2.14	11
Travel	1.76	18	1.86	18
High School Sports	1.73	19	1.85	19

age of 30. The most promising targets, therefore, are those people closest to the threshold at which they will become readers regardless of what the editor does. Efforts to tip them into the category of newspaper readers a year or even a few months ahead of schedule should be more cost-effective than going for the younger people who are still some years away from the lifestyle patterns associated with regular newspaper reading.

The target-group model, while susceptible to the same defects as the referendum model, has one enormous advantage: the usefulness of its results can be tested. An editor who follows the basic referendum model and then sees readership go up or down cannot easily isolate a cause-effect relationship because so many intervening variables outside his control can also have an effect on readership.

When a particular and identifiable group is the target, however, it is often reasonable to assume that the intervening variables fall on target and nontarget persons alike. So if the editorial strategy is working, the ratio of target to nontarget readers should increase.

For most newspaper organizations, however, this is not an advantage, because few have their research efforts organized along sufficiently long time horizons to provide the continuity needed for such post-testing and evaluation.

A Prioritization Model

Another step toward a less informal and more explicit model was taken in research for Knight-Ridder editors. The basic editor's quandary involves choices among competing elements for space in the news hole. The researcher's goal is to give the editor usable information for making those choices. This prioritization model employs the same basic information used in the referendum or target-group models plus one additional factor whose utility is exceeded only by its obviousness: whether or not the topic being considered has something to do with newspaper readership.

In interpreting the referenda in Table 2, it is worth noting that the question was asked in a context of making judgments about newspapers and their content. Responses are therefore colored by what the respondent is accustomed to finding in the newspaper. That world events rank so much higher in interest than household repairs may be in part because respondents expect to find information about world affairs in a newspaper, while they are not accustomed to looking into a newspaper for help in doing household repairs. For a newspaper to market itself as a source of the latter type of information requires some retraining of readers and potential readers. Before undertaking such an effort, it would be helpful to know how difficult or how necessary such retraining might be.

It is therefore important to find the extent to which interest in each of the nineteen topics on the list is already associated with newspaper reading. If a large proportion of the potential audience is interested in a topic and if interest in the topic is associated with reading a newspaper, it is fairly safe to assume that the subject area is well enough covered to protect circulation. Questions about the direction of causation may be postponed. Whether the person's interest in the subject drives him to the newspaper or whether having the newspaper makes him interested in the subject, the outcome is the same: the newspaper has served and is serving that customer.

On the other hand, if a large proportion of the audience is interested in a topic and if the interest in that topic is *not* associated with newspaper reading (or, as happens rarely, if interest is negatively associated with reading), the newspaper has an opportunity to create a new clientele.

The point is best made by illustration. Consider the case of national politics, one of the highest-ranking topics. Interest in national politics is strongly associated with newspaper reading in the four-city survey (Table 3). For an editor, the indicated treatment of this topic is a maintaining strategy. What he or she is doing with this topic works, so it might as well be continued.

Now consider another high-interest topic, consumer information. Interest in this topic does not appear to be very strongly associated with newspaper reading (Table 4). Here is an area, therefore, that may be ripe for development. The development could take the form of expanded coverage of consumer news, promotion of the existing coverage, or both.

It is now apparent that we are dealing with a classification scheme for newsworthy topics and that this scheme involves four property spaces (Figure 2). A decision rule can be formulated for each of the spaces. We have already figured out the decision rules for spaces A and B. Recapitulating them and proposing rules for the remaining spaces, we have:

A. Maintain: This high interest, positive-association category includes the subjects for which the editor is doing things right. People are interested in these subjects, and the greater their interest, the more they read the newspaper. A maintenance of effort is called for.

TABLE 3

Interest in National Politics

	High	Low	Total
Readers	63%	38%	41%
Nonreaders	37	62	59
N = 1,128	100	100	100

TABLE 4

Interest in Consumer Information

	High	Low	Total
Readers	40%	43%	41%
Nonreaders	60	57	59
N = 1,128	100	100	100

B. Watch: Subjects with low interest but high association with readership may be important. They could represent small but important market segments whose coverage should, at the very least, be maintained. When the interests tend to have low duplication with other interests, they should be considered candidates for enhanced coverage. The cumulative effect of such narrow topics can be important.

C. Push: Where interest is high but not associated with readership, the editor's opportunity for attracting new readers is the greatest. Such subjects can be covered with target groups in mind or they can be directed at readers in general. When they are already covered, that coverage should be promoted.

D. Pass: If interest in a subject is low, and if what interest there is has little or no association with newspaper reading, an editor would do well to pass over it in favor of areas where an effort will produce a greater chance of return.

The 19 subjects in the 4-city survey were classified according to the following criteria. The association between readership and interest in a topic was considered positive if the gamma value in a 3x2 table (3 categories of interest against readership and nonreadership) was .1 or greater. If you have never heard of a "gamma value" before, don't worry about it. It is a simple test of the strength of a relationship between 2 things that vary. If they vary together, i.e., if one goes up when the other goes up (or down), gamma is a relatively big number. If they are not related at all, gamma is 0. In this particular case, the sample size was sufficient to produce an approximate significance level of .05 or better when gamma was at least .1. This means that we are probably looking at something real and not just sucking our thumbs over random sampling variation. Interest was classified as high if the mean score was at least 2 (equivalent to "somewhat interested").

Readers who have followed historic trends in newspaper marketing will here recognize support for increasing the essentiality of newspapers through service features. The topics in the space identified as presenting the greatest opportunity (identified as C in Figure 2) deal mainly with service and self-improvement. On the other hand, traditional subjects that newspapers have usually done best fall, with happy predictability, in the A cell, where a maintaining strategy is called for. The model, in short, produces a result that is intuitively satisfying.

This basic notion—that readership can be gained by pushing service features—was arrived at by a lot of editors in the 1970s without any help from research models. But those who arrived at it intuitively often made a mistake from which the formal model might have protected them. These editors took off in pursuit of soft content and service features with such enthusiasm that they sacrificed traditional hard news content to make room for stories about how to paint your kitchen yellow and the like.

FIGURE 2

Persons 25–29 in the Four Markets Combined

	High Interest	Low Interest
Readership Associated	*A* World Events National Politics Local Issues State Government Pro Sports	*B* Travel Gardening School Board
Not Associated	*C* Consumer Advice Crime Budget Stretching Food Child Rearing College Sports Leisure	*D* Coping High School Sports Household Repairs Home Decorating

None of the data discussed in this chapter say that you can do that and get away with it. Indeed, their message is quite the contrary: hard news works, and you cut it back at your peril. Keep giving it to your readers, the model says, and then, if you can find the resources to give them something else, consider service features. It may indeed be possible to divert some fraction of resources from hard news to innovative content at a net gain, but the risk is very high and no research has been devised that can predict what the net gain or loss will be or what the optimum fraction of diversion might be. Only trial and error can discover that. And the prudent editor will find a way to try new things without cannibalizing the very categories that do the most for readership as identified by the formal model.

The example given here uses data from four markets. The temptation is perhaps inevitable to examine the four markets individually to see how stable the categorizations might be. Sampling error becomes more of a problem at this level, but the same general pattern holds for all four markets. Some departures from the central pattern are readily explained by local differences. One of the markets, for example, is primarily a college town, and in that market, interest in college sports moves from the C category to category A, as would be expected if the newspaper were doing a good job of covering college sports.

The lines that separate the property spaces in Figure 2 are, of course, thin ones. And the method for measuring reader interest is, as we all know, subject to questions of validity. We may not always get honest answers from the reader who likes to think he cares about world affairs but spends his time with the sports page. Nevertheless, assumptions must be made and lines must be drawn for the work of analysis and priority-setting to go forward. An editor intent on improving a newspaper must start somewhere, and an orderly means of choosing the starting point is often helpful. Some formalization of mental models can provide that help in an intuitively satisfying and nonthreatening way.

A linear regression model sounds like something fairly formidable, but you come across them in newspapers all the time. Here's an example from the top of a lead story in *USA Today*:

> Higher home mortgage rates, which have crept up to about 14.5 percent on conventional loans since May, have frozen out more than 900,000 potential buyers, housing official estimated Wednesday.
>
> And, some 225,000 to 250,000 buyers will quit looking for houses each time rates climb another half-percentage point, said Bill Adkinson of the National Association of Realtors.

Any such observation about a given change in one variable—in this case, home mortgage rates—causing a given change in another—number of potential buyers—is a statement of a linear regression model. It is linear because the same amount of change in the independent variable always leads to the same amount of change in the dependent variable. If you think of it as a line on a graph, that line will be straight. If you think of it as an equation, it will always take this general form:

$$Y = C + Xb$$

Put the mortgage example into this equation, and it looks like this:

$$\text{Number of discouraged buyers} = 900,000 + .005 * 237,500$$

The C in the equation is a constant that anchors the line to a starting point somewhere. The story tells us that the reference point is the 900,000 buyers already "frozen out." The rest of the equation describes the steepness of the slope.

We can make this easier to visualize by starting with a simple scatterplot. Consider this hypothesis (the newspaper and the data are fictitious): street sales of the *Miami Journal* pick up whenever a hurricane is spotted near the Cape Verde islands; and they tend to increase by some uniform amount as the distance between Miami and the hurricane decreases.

From circulation records, we collect eight data points:

Distance	Sales
1,035	2,000
805	3,000
667	4,000
529	4,000
460	6,000
391	8,000
276	7,000
115	8,000

Sure enough, just by scanning the columns we can see that street sales increase as the hurricane gets closer to Miami. But for an even clearer picture we need a plot. We'll show street sales on the vertical or Y axis and miles on the horizontal or X axis (Figure 3).

How to describe what is going on here? We could say that it looks like the profile of an alligator peering out of a swamp. Or that it resembles the Florida Keys in mirror image. Or that it is a pretty good approximation to a straight line. When we take the latter approach, we are invoking something called the general linear model, of which simple linear regression is the principal component.

The model enables us to be quite specific in our description. Any good statistics text will give you the formula for least-squares regression, which can be used to find and describe the straight line that best fits these data points. Or you can skip the formula and have a computer do the work for you—or even a low-cost pocket calculator, such as the TI-55. In this case, the best-fitting straight line is described by the following equation:

$$Y = 9,150 - 7.3 * X$$

For most of us, words are easier. Try this: when the hurricane hits, the *Miami Journal* will sell 9,150 additional papers on the street. Before it hits, 7.3 fewer papers will be sold for each mile of distance between Miami and the hurricane.

Now that would be true, of course, only if all the data points were always right on the line. In fact, they are not. But because they tend to fit a straight line, the linear model becomes a practical tool for planning

FIGURE 3

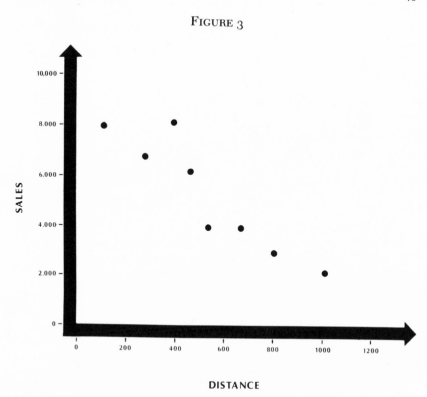

DISTANCE

purposes, especially if the variation around the straight line is random. If it is, then the straight line becomes the best guess available, and we can almost hear the circulation manager saying, "Let's see, the hurricane is 500 miles away, and 500 times 7.3 is 3,650 and 9,150 minus 3,650 is 5,500. Okay, Harry, let's up the street edition press run by 5,500."

Before using this tool, the circulation manager might want some quantifiable indication of how well the linear model fits the data at hand. The statistic telling us that is the correlation coefficient, also yielded by the formula for least squares regression. In this case, the correlation coefficient, also known as Pearsonian r, is $-.930$. How to interpret it? If the correlation were 1 or -1, it would mean that all of the data points were sitting right on the straight line. A positive value means that the line slopes upward to the right; i.e., an increase in X yields an increase in Y. A

FIGURE 4

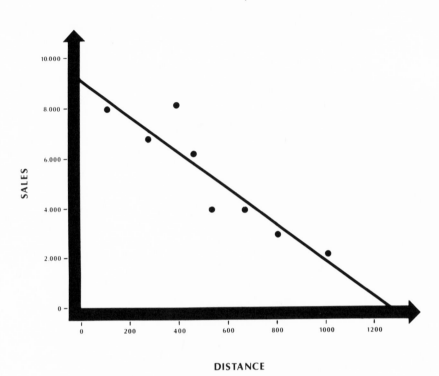

DISTANCE

negative value, which we have here, indicates a downward slope to the
right: as X increases, Y decreases. A correlation coefficient of o would
mean that the data do not fit a straight line at all. They still might be in
some easily-described pattern. They could form an O or a U or maybe an
S, and the pattern might have some predictive value. But it would not fit
a linear model.

The correlation coefficient has another useful interpretation. Its square
is the amount of variance explained. This concept is so important that we
are going to elaborate on it a little bit. First we'll look at our plot again
with the best-fitting straight line drawn in (Figure 4).

This line is called the "least squares line" because it, out of all possible
straight lines, is the one with the least total of squared vertical distances

from each data point to the line. We can illustrate these least squares distances by drawing them in (Figure 5).

Those vertical lines are the physical representation of unexplained variance. The better the fit that the dots make to the line, the less the unexplained variance. If all the dots were on the line, we could say in plain English, "All of the variation in added street sales can be explained by the hurricane's distance from Miami." As it is, we can say that 86% of the variation is explained.

But wait, you say. Every percent has to have a base somewhere. Where is the base here? Good point. I haven't shown you what we mean by variance. Let's look at the plot again with some different vertical lines (Figure 6). These show the total variance.

FIGURE 5

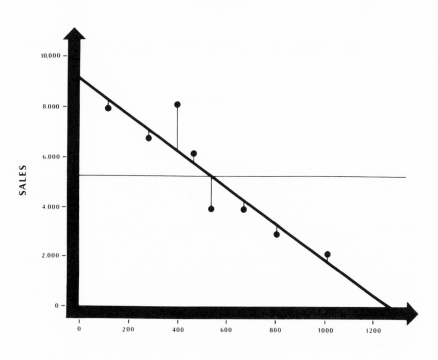

DISTANCE

FIGURE 6

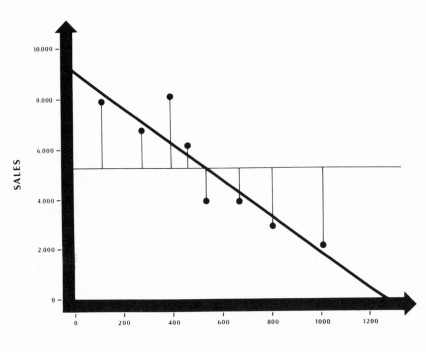

DISTANCE

This time, the vertical line runs from each data point to a horizontal line representing the mean of Y. Why? Well, suppose you are the circulation manager of the *Miami Journal* and you know a hurricane is coming, but you haven't figured out that its distance from Miami has an effect on sales. All you know is that you sell more papers when there is a hurricane than when there isn't. How many more? Well, it varies. But your average over 8 data points, ranging from 8,000 copies to 2,000 copies, is 5,250. So if you wanted to minimize your risk of being wrong, and if you had nothing else to go on, you would use that average—the mean, to be more precise about it—as your guess.

And—here's the good part—the measure of your error is the extent to which there is *variance* around that mean.

Now a market researcher comes along, he or she explains the general linear model to you, and a least squares line is found to fit the available data. Now you are smarter: instead of using the average across the 8 data points to make your prediction, you use the regression line. If you had been given the equation for the line before the 8 events forming these data points had occurred, your guesses would be much better than if you had just used the mean. How much better? If you measure the distance between each data point and the mean and add those distances up, you'll see how well you did using that way of guessing. Now measure the difference between each data point and the regression line. You've done a lot better. And if you calculate the ratio of those 2 sums, you will find that your guesses were 86% better—that is, the total squared distance between the estimates and the reality was reduced by 86% when you used the regression line. And that's why a statistician will tell you that distance of the hurricane from Miami explains 86% of the variance in added street sales.

The Unexplained Variance

That's pretty good, but the persistent researcher is troubled by the thought of that 14% of the variance that remains unexplained. Is there any way to reduce it? Yes, because there may be yet another variable for which a measure can be obtained that will further increase the explanatory or predictive power of the model. Wind speed, perhaps. A hurricane with top wind speeds of 150 MPH ought to sell more papers than one that blows at a mere 80 MPH, don't you think?

Here's how that information is cranked into the equation. For each data point, we measure the difference between its observed value and the value predicted by the model (represented by the physical distance on the plot from the point to the regression line). This difference is expressed in units of Y, or, in this case, in terms of numbers of papers. If we sold more than the model predicted, the difference is positive. If less, it is negative. This difference is called the *residual* and it is the real-world manifestation of unexplained variance. It is what we have left to explain. This residual is what we want our new equation to predict.

So we could make another pair of columns of numbers. Y would be the residual from the previous model. And X would be the new independent (or predictor) variable, the speed of the wind in miles per hour. And if it worked, we could make another profound statement, which would go something like this: the additional street sales will equal 9,150 papers plus or minus some other constant introduced by the second step of this regression, minus 7.3 papers for each mile the hurricane is from Miami, plus X papers for each MPH of wind speed. And what you will have done is shown the effect of the new variable, after the effect of the first variable is already accounted for or, as we say, controlled.

Stepwise multiple regression does something like this, only better. It gives you an equation with this form:

$$Y = C + b_1 * X_1 + b_2 * X_2 + b_3 * X_3 \ldots$$

The coefficients or b's are estimates of the effect of each of the different independent variables (X's) on Y when all of the other independent variables are controlled. For the equation to work best, you need independent variables that are not correlated with one another. This assumption is often violated, however. In our hurricane example, it is violated because hurricanes originating around Cape Verde tend to increase their wind speed as they move west. When there is such intercorrelation there really is no way to sort out the independent effects of each variable. As a practical matter, however, you may improve the predictive power of the equation by adding variables that have some correlation with one another. If predicting the value of Y is more important to you than estimating the effect of individual variables in the casual chain, then it makes sense to go ahead.

Evaluating Circulation Performance

Here is a real-life example. The *Philadelphia Inquirer,* fighting a vigorous competitive battle in the 1970s, wanted to evaluate its circulation performance in small geographic areas.

The traditional way to do that is to color a map. One color code is used for average circulation penetration (circulation divided by households), another for areas below average, and a third for those above average. Or there might be five colors to allow for areas that are *way* above or below average. The editor and the circulation director look at the map, their eyes are drawn to the below-average areas, and they notice that these are mostly low-income areas where they shouldn't expect to be average. And they look at the above-average places on the map and observe that older, affluent citizens live there, and that explains that. In short, the map does not help very much.

What they really need is a way to evaluate those small areas that measures circulation performance against the potential—with the potential based on the known demographic characteristics. Stepwise multiple regression is tailor-made for that kind of a problem, but you need two things: census data and circulation data based on the census areas.

In the Philadelphia case, circulation data were available for geographic units based on the census bureau's minor civil divisons. Demographic data for each of these units, plus circulation and household count, were fed into the model. Out came an equation with a multiple regression coefficient of .795 that explained 63% of the variance in *Philadelphia Inquirer* household penetration. These are the variables that did the trick, along with their coefficients:

Variable	Coefficient
Percent working in Philadelphia	.15
Percent with income of $15,000 and up	.40
Percent older families	1.56
Suburban paper penetration	− .06
Population density index	.12
New housing index	.21
Percent single females	1.54
Percent auto commuters	.19
Percent white	.12
Percent childless families	− .55
Percent younger families	.76

And the regression constant was − .35. So the model tells us that for any given small geographic area, you can predict the circulation penetration of the *Philadelphia Inquirer* with 66% better accuracy than you can by using the mean if you have the variables listed above. And to arrive at the prediction, you start with − .35 and add .15 of a percentage point for each 1% who work in Philadelphia plus .4% for each 1% with incomes of $15,000 and up, and so on.

Some of it, you may notice, does not make sense. Why should *Inquirer* penetration go up if there are a lot of older families and then go up some more if there are a lot of younger families? Blame the multicolinearity problem. The exact contribution of each variable just can't be teased out when variables are intercorrelated. It doesn't matter so much in this application, because what we want to know is how much circulation penetration to expect in each place once the demographics have been accounted for. So we get the computer to print us out a table of residuals.

The residual, you will remember, is the difference, for each data point, between the observed value and the value predicted by the equation. And to discover that difference is the whole point of the exercise. Here is a portion of the table of residuals that the computer supplied:

Unit	Predicted	Observed	Residual
01A	.37	.41	.04
01B	.41	.41	.0
01C	.35	.41	.06
02A	.38	.39	.01
02B	.36	.39	.03
02C	.36	.39	.03
02D	.35	.39	.04
03A	.40	.30	−.10
04A	.39	.34	−.05
04B	.27	.34	.07
05A	.36	.25	−.11
06A	.58	.43	−.15

You can see the value of it. In district 06A, for example, the 43% penetration looks good compared to the rest of the area until you see what the regression model predicts. And that makes you want to dig further into what is happening there to see if anything can be done to bring the area up to its circulation potential. The study uncovered a number of places with high unrealized potential in the suburbs around Philadelphia.

Another Application

Studies by the Newspaper Advertising Bureau have shown that readers report more interest in national news than in news about state and local government. In some cases, world news also ranks higher than most categories of state and local news (Bogart, 1981).

This finding has run counter to the intuition of many editors, who tend to believe the textbook maxim that the closer a story is to home, the more interesting it is to the reader. However, many single-market proprietary studies have also shown that national and international news is rated higher in interest than local news. The NAB study has the advantage of measuring direct response to specific newspaper stories. Respondents were shown copies of their own newspapers and asked to rate the content that was later classified by the researchers.

Editors' discomfort with these findings has led to several attempts to check or explain them. Ruth Clark (1979) in her focus groups found "a surprisingly strong interest in national and international news." However, she said, "the focus group findings suggest that readers do not, in fact, want more national and international news than local reporting."

Joe Belden and John Schweitzer (1978) suspected that readers might rate national stories higher because editors give them better play. They tried to separate the subject matter from the context of the front page by asking respondents to evaluate headlines that were identical except for the location to which they referred—"this town," "this county," "this city," "U.S. cities," or "world's cities." They found that, no matter what the substance of the headline, interest decreased as distance increased. This study was conducted among people who stopped subscribing to the newspaper in a suburb of a major city. While they may not be representative, the findings strongly support the suspicion that news play, not content, made the national stories in the NAB survey more interesting. Here again we see the old dilemma of whether a newspaper mirrors or molds public attitudes.

At Knight-Ridder Newspapers, an opportunity arose to tackle this problem on behavioral rather than the more slippery attitudinal grounds. It was decided, in other words, not to ask people what interests them, but to observe which kinds of stories appear to stimulate the decision to purchase the newspaper.

The data base was a sample of 462 weekdays in 1977 and 1978. For each day, single-copy sales of the *Philadelphia Inquirer* were recorded as the dependent variable; data were also collected for 33 other variables, some dealing with newspaper content and others describing the external environment, such as the weather, which we thought might have something to do with street sales on any given day. We were aware that most attempts to relate content to street sales—some of them our own—had been fruitless. So many different things happen to affect the sales of any given issue that it is very difficult to sort out the effect of one variable from the confusing multitude. Clearly, some heavier analytical artillery was needed than is found in the usual newspaper study.

The technique chosen was to fit these variables to a multiple linear regression model. A regression equation, as we have seen, simply describes the changes in a variable associated with a given amount of change in another variable. For example, the statement that street sales decrease by 0.1% for each inch of new snow on the ground is a regression equation expressed in words. A multiple regression equation does the same thing, but gives the benefit of showing how a succession of variables can add to or substract from the thing in which one is interested. In a refinement of this technique, it is possible to use simple binary variables—those that can be expressed with a value of either 0 or 1—in the equation. A mass-transit strike provided us with an example of a binary variable. The strike was either on or it was off. When it was on, street sales dropped by 6%.

Recall now that the usefulness of a regression equation is measured by how much of the variability in the dependent variable—in this case single copy sales—is explained or "predicted" by the equation. "Prediction" is used here in the scientific sense and does not mean that we claim to be able to foretell the future. It merely means that, looking back over our accumulated data, we can say that had we had this equation at the beginning of our string of 462 weekdays, we could have used it to predict street sales on any given day with some specified degree of accuracy. Making predictions from today forward is, of course, much more difficult.

After trying various combinations of variables, we came up with a multiple regression equation that used 21 independent variables to explain 54% of the variance in single-copy sales. This means that using the equation to guess the street sales for a particular day would produce results that are 54% better than we would obtain by basing our guess on the average street sale.

What about the other 46% of the variance? It remains unexplained. Perhaps it could be explained by other variables we have not yet thought to identify and measure. Or perhaps the existing variables would explain it if we could discover and identify some nonlinear effects and adjust for them. Without special adjustments, the regression equation assumes that the effect of one variable on another always proceeds in a straight-line fashion; i. e., the first inch of snow reduces single copy sales by exactly the same amount as, say, the 24th inch of snow.

This assumption will not always be true. Sometimes one can improve the predictive power of a regression equation by identifying those variables whose effect is not linear and reexpressing them so that the linear model will fit. For example, if the effect of snow diminishes as the amount of snow increases, a fit to a linear model might be made by reexpressing the inches of snowfall by their square root or their logarithm.

In academic studies, attention is usually focused on the relative explanatory power of different variables. Academicians are interested in building general theories to explain human behavior, and they want to do it in the most parsimonious way. The way to do that is to explain a lot of variance with a few variables. In action-oriented research, we are more interested in estimating the practical effect of those variables that are in some degree controllable by managers. We can't control snowfall, but we can control the content of page one, the number and kinds of sales promotions, and perhaps a few other variables. And, if we can produce an equation with high predictive power, we might even use it to decide how many newspapers to distribute to specific locations on a given day. But mainly we want to know how the number of newspapers sold will change as we make certain managerial decisions.

Of the 21 independent variables in our model, 13 had effects on circulation that were significantly different from 0. In other words, we could be quite sure that each of these variables had an effect on circulation, and that we knew the direction of the effect. We could tell which policies would help and which would hurt. The model also gives us estimates of the amount of effect along with confidence intervals for assessing the accuracy of the estimates.

The variables that explained the most variance were those that can't be controlled, most notably season and day of the week. We fitted the seasonal variable to the linear model by plotting single-copy sales against time to identify seasonal peaks and valleys. We then created 3 newspaper buying seasons by identifying the high points, the low points, and those in between, cutting them so that each of the 3 categories had about the same number of days. This 3-category variable was then treated as a continuous variable, with values from 1 to 3.

The variable with the second-highest explanatory power was day of the week. Actually, this was 4 variables. We had only the 5 weekdays in our sample, and 4 of these 5 were used to create binary variables, each with a value of 1 or 0. A variable for the 5th day would, of course, have been redundant, because of all if the first 4 are 0, identification of the remaining day is automatic. Street sales on the highest day were about 8% better than those on the lowest day. The seasonal variable and 1 of the day variables together accounted for more than 30% of the variance.

For those who insist on knowing what the equation looks like, here it is:

$$Y = 79 + 5 * X_1 + 5.5 * X_2 - 0.1 * X_3 - 6.3 * X_4 + 1.3 * X_5$$
$$+ 1.3 * X_6 + 1.1 * X_7 - 1.9 * X_8 + 0 * X_9 + 2.3 * X_{10} - 0.8 * X_{11}$$
$$- 0 * X_{12} - 0.5 * X_{13} - 0.4 * X_{14} + 1.8 * X_{15} + 2.3 * X_{16} + 2.2 * X_{17}$$
$$+ 2.4 * X_{18} + 2.1 * X_{19} - 3.6 * X_{20} - 0.1 * X_{21}$$

The Y stands for predicted single-copy sales. The equation starts from a base of 79% of average street sales. I won't define all of the 21 variables, but I shall describe some of the more interesting ones. The seasonal variable I have just described is X_1, and the equation tells us that you can add 5% to the base if it is the lowest selling season, 10% if it is the next-best season, and 15% if it is the best season. The next variable, X_2, stands for a particular day of the week when advertising is heavy. If today is that day, add 5.5% of the average circulation to the equation. Next is X_3, which represents the number of inches of snow on the ground. It tells us the circulation falls by .1% for each inch of snow. After that, we have a binary variable representing the previously mentioned strike, and it says that if the strike was on, street sales were down 6.3% from the average.

Each of the variables that I have described so far, with the exception of X_3, inches of snowfall, is statistically significant at the .001 level or better, meaning that the odds are less than 1 in 1000 that a larger sample of days would steer us in some other direction. To put it another way, the probability is very high that the effects are not 0 and that they are in the indicated direction.

Now we come to the variable dealing with the question that opened this discussion. The variable labeled X_5 is a binary variable telling us about the content of the lead story for the day. If it was national or international, the value is 1, and if it was state or local, the value is 0. The equation tells us that a national story will improve street sales by 1.3% above the average. This advantage is statistically significant at the .014 level, meaning that the probability is less than 2% that a larger sample would show national news having no effect or hurting sales. Now, a 1.3% improvement in street sales may seem small. But when you consider the average variation of street sales from day to day, it becomes much more impressive. It represents a number of additional newspapers that we would clearly prefer to sell if given the opportunity.

This brings us to the more difficult question of how to act on this research. If research reports had to be written on bumper stickers, we might be tempted to say, "Avoid local news" and spread the word to editors to lead with national stories whenever possible. But that would be the wrong response. A more complicated explanation of what we have found is required.

There are two ways, equally logical, to explain it. One is that national news is indeed intrinsically better than local news. The other is that local and national news have equal appeal, but that editors are biased in favor of local news.

The second has greater intuitive appeal to those who write and edit news. If it is true, then the research described here becomes a useful device for fine-tuning an editor's sensibilities about what to select for page one. It is easier to appreciate this application if we ask ourselves what the research would have shown if editors always made perfect decisions and chose the story with the best drawing power regardless of its subject matter. The answer is obvious enough. Assuming a constant supply of both local and national stories that are candidates for page one display, and assuming that the editor always chooses the best story regardless of content, the difference between national and local would be zero.

If this is not obvious, imagine two barrels filled with news stories. One barrel contains local stories, stacked in order of their attractiveness to single-copy buyers. They are also graded so that the most attractive stories, those at the top of the barrel, are graded 100, while the least attractive stories at the bottom are graded 0. The other barrel, of course, contains graded and ordered national stories. The rational editor will choose the story with the highest grade no matter from which barrel he has to draw to get it. If he looks in the local barrel and finds that the best story is a 90, he will check the national barrel for a 91. If he has a plentiful supply of 100s in the national barrel and not in the local barrel, he will avoid the local barrel until its supply of 100s is replenished or until the level of quality in the national barrel is lowered to the level of the local barrel. The long-term effect of this rational decision making is that the attractiveness of the local and national stories that appear in the newspaper will be, on the average, equal. And the regression weights, in the process we have described above, would tend toward 0.

Now the usefulness of regression analysis as a tool for fine tuning becomes apparent. The difference in pulling power of local and national stories in the sample period was significant in the statistical sense, but not as impressive in a substantive sense. In other words, the editors were coming pretty close to the optimum mix. Their only flaw was a mild bias toward local stories. The only way that national stories could outpull local stories to any measurable extent would be for inferior local stories to get into the paper. That can happen if editors are biased in favor of local stories. It is a very slight bias in this case, and one almost hesitates to bring it up at all for fear of instigating an overcorrection. But such studies can, especially if done regularly, help editors to navigate among the competing ambiguities they face every day and initiate an occasional steering correction.

Let us assume that the premise underlying this plea for a fine-tuned adjustment toward national news is wrong. That premise, you will recall, is that the pulling power of the two categories of news is basically equal, and that editors' prejudice gives local news more of a burden than it can carry. What happens if that premise is wrong?

The rival premise leads, fortunately enough, to the same action. The rival premise is that national news sells more papers because it is intrinsically a better drawing card than local news—not much better, but a little better, 1.3% better, on the average.

If that premise is the correct one, the uncertain editor still has a guide. When all other factors seem to be equal, he or she should choose from the barrel with the best sales record. Again, the message is to fine-tune the decision process with a small adjustment toward national news.

The greatest contribution of this approach, however, may be to serve as a reminder to avoid bumper-sticker thinking. Many small corrections are better than a few spasmodic changes. As far as the national-versus-local issue is concerned, it is hard to improve on the summary of the editor for whom this research was done. Gene Roberts said, without using a single word of research jargon: "Editors who automatically think that local is best are dumb-ass editors. People respond to a given story despite what the category is."

Experimental Designs / 6.

An experimental study is one in which the investigator manipulates the environment beyond what is necessary for simple measurement. An experiment can be conducted in a laboratory setting or in the field. Experimental manipulation can be done in survey research by presenting different stimuli to different groups of respondents.

In advertising research, there is a long and well-established tradition of experimental research to show what kinds of messages and what kinds of delivery produce the best results. One of the classics is a study of the effects of color in advertising conducted by a newspaper in Long Beach, California, in 1959. Before examining how that study was designed, let's think about some of the possible ways you could test for the effectiveness of color in advertising.

The simplest test would be to run a color ad for a given store and then go to that store and ask the manager if any improvement in sales was noticed. A lot of research is done that way, but you can see its weakness. To measure an improvement, you need a baseline for comparison. So measure the store at two times: once when there has been a color ad and at another time when the ad has been in black and white:

Time 1   Color
Time 2   B & W

If color works, sales should be greater at Time 1 than Time 2. But you can see the flaw. Lots of other things besides the color in the advertising could have changed between Time 1 and Time 2 to cause a change in sales. Perhaps what we really need is to compare two stores at the same time:

Store 1   Store 2
Color   B & W

But that doesn't quite do it because you won't be able to find two stores that are exactly alike in all respects except for the use of color in advertising. If Store 1 has more sales, it might be because more traffic happened to be on its street that day.

The solution, of course, is to combine the two designs so that time and store are varied simultaneously. For good measure, the Long Beach paper replicated the design twice, using three kinds of stores. What it came up with was this:

	Jewelry Stores		Furniture Stores		Variety Stores	
	Store 1	Store 2	Store 1	Store 2	Store 1	Store 2
Time 1:	Color	B & W	Color	B & W	Color	B & W
Time 2:	B & W	Color	B & W	Color	B & W	Color

This is called a Latin Square design. Actually, it is three Latin Squares, one for each type of store. Both store and time are controlled. Of course, there are still potential problems. If color is extremely effective in selling jewelry, Store 1 might soak up all the potential demand at Time 1, leaving no business for Store 2 when it uses color at Time 2. It pays to do it in widely scattered locations.

When this study was first done in Long Beach, it showed a decisive advantage for color. When attempts were made to replicate it in later years, color had apparently lost its clear advantage.

Measuring Design Effects

Attempts have been made to transfer this technique to newspaper circulation questions, but without very clear results. In 1978, the *Tallahassee Democrat* tested the effect of page-one color on single-copy sales. Two groups of newsracks were chosen. The press run was split, and on the first day, Group 1 got color on the front page and Group 2 got black and white. The next day, the treatment was reversed. This alternating pattern continued for two and a half weeks.

The result was a statistically insignificant difference in favor of the black and white. That version sold 3,031 copies to the color fronts' 2,950. Why didn't color have the expected effect?

Tallahassee is a one-paper town with very loyal readers. Single-copy readers have a well-fixed habit of dropping their coins in the racks, and it takes a more earth-shaking change than color or its lack to modify that habit. Over time, color might very well make a difference by drawing new readers to the racks at a greater rate than before. A cumulative effect might be measurable where a day-to-day effect was not.

The effect of design changes is extremely hard to measure, no matter what the method. The *Boston Globe* prepared five different versions of the front page for April 1, 1976, and asked readers in a survey which they preferred. They ranged from very traditional with a high story count to modern and modular with a low story count backed up by a column of briefs. The winner, with a resounding plurality, was the most traditional design, which shocked the managers because this was a design that the paper had abandoned two years before. The existing design, basically traditional but with a low story count, came in second. The radical changes got only fragmentary support. This is a story that has been repeated at many newspapers, and the moral is that design changes have to be sold to the readers carefully and slowly. And they have to be rationalized on some basis other than what the readers think they want, because the readers always want what is familiar. If a new design is more functional, if it makes it possible for the reader to navigate through the paper more efficiently, it can certainly be justified on that ground alone and needs no referendum to ratify it. Readers will come to appreciate it in time, as they learn to use it.

The Effect of Content

Content is another matter. The Philadelphia regression model described in the previous chapter shows that what the front page says, rather than how it says it, makes a difference in street sales. Philadelphia may also have been a better town to test this in than Tallahassee because of its highly competitive situation at the time. In Philadelphia there were more people who decided to put some money in a newspaper coin box but postponed the decision on which paper to buy until they scanned the front pages. The Philadelphia study was a natural experiment. Nothing was manipulated beyond what was necessary to make the observations, but the observations were structured to pick up on changing conditions that were happening naturally—nature's manipulations, if you will.

It is possible to evaluate content in small group situations that come close to being experiments. When Knight-Ridder was evaluating potential creators of a new feature for children, small groups of children were presented with three competing prototypes to evaluate. To establish a baseline, they were also asked to evaluate a well-established existing feature for children. To control for order effects, the order of presentation was rotated so that each feature was first, second, third, and fourth in the lineup an equal number of times. The Dynamite Kids' Page, which was eventually adopted, was a clear winner across a great variety of small groups in different locations.

Surveys as Experiments

A survey can be used to experiment or to simulate an experiment. Imagine the following problem. You are the publisher of a newspaper and you have some money to spend on improvements. You want to spend the first dollars where they do the most good in circulation retention, i.e., keeping the present readers. Two of your department heads, the editor and the circulation manager, have made equally compelling arguments that the money should be spent on their departments. How do you decide where you can get the most bang for the buck?

A survey done for the *Journal of Commerce* in 1975 took a shot at this problem. It was a mail survey to both present and former readers. Both groups were asked which of a long list of standing features they read and how useful each was to them. They were also asked about the promptness of delivery service.

A regression model was fitted using those two variables—number of features declared useful and promptness of delivery—to predict retention. It wasn't really a prediction, of course, because all the data were collected after the fact. The people who had dropped the paper might have been giving rationalizations instead of information that would really be useful in prediction. But we had the data in hand and the computer didn't care when it was collected, so we tried the model anyway. Sure enough, it produced an equation that could be interpreted as yielding a probability of retaining the paper based on the number of useful features read and delivery timing. Such an equation, if you truly believe in it, can be used for simulating a management decision and predicting the result.

Thinking of adding some editorial features? Okay. Assume from other data collected in the survey that 10 percent of the readers in the sample would have added one of the new features to their useful lists. Tell the computer to increment the number of useful features read by 1 for a random 10%. Or, if you have a good idea which of your readers will like a planned feature, put in the increment for those specific cases. Now run every case through the equation and average the result. Since this result is expressed as a probability, you can average the individual probabilities and translate the result into an estimate of the number of readers who will be retained.

A similar estimate can be obtained for the result of an alternate possibility, say paying for airborne courier services to ensure next-day delivery in distant cities. Since one element in the equation is delivery time, you tell the computer to advance that by a given amount for selected classes of cases. Run the equation again, and you have an estimate of the benefit from that policy.

This is not exactly a success story, because the data from the *Journal of Commerce* survey, with its one-shot design and reliance on respondent recall for the attitudes they held before they made the retention decision, were not clean enough for such a high-powered procedure. But I cite it to show how simple a computer simulation can be, once you have the data. The barrier is not computer power or mathematical skill but collection of good enough data. So let us turn to that subject.

Data for Simulation Problems

To start with, you need a way to sort cause from effect. A one-shot cross-sectional study isn't very good at that. For example, there is a strong positive correlation between liking "Dick Tracy" and number of years as a regular reader. That is interesting, but it doesn't tell you whether "Dick Tracy" is a cause or an effect. A reader of many years will have had more chances to become addicted to "Dick Tracy" through random wanderings in the newspaper than someone who has been a reader for a shorter period, so longevity could cause "Dick Tracy" readership. Moreover, "Dick Tracy" is a dramatic serial that you have to follow every day to understand, and the older readers, being more regular, are in a better position to do that. On the other hand, maybe some people read the paper on a given day just so they can find out what "Dick Tracy" is doing now.

To complicate matters even more, both longevity of readership and liking for "Dick Tracy" could be caused by some undiscovered third factor. Or they could be both part cause and part effect in varying degrees for different people. To even begin to sort all of this out, you need a survey incorporated into an experiment with a longitudinal design.

A longitudinal design is one that measures whatever it measures at 2 different times. And it can tell you whether a particular phenomenon is predominantly cause or effect. The trick is called "cross-lagged correlation," and here is how it works. Suppose that you have a measure of liking for "Dick Tracy" and readership longevity for 2 widely separated times, say the summers of 1974 and 1984. That gives you 6 possible things to correlate. Here's how:

$$
\begin{array}{ccc}
1974 & & 1984 \\
\text{a. Tracy Score} & \longleftrightarrow & \text{c. Tracy Score} \\
\updownarrow & \times & \updownarrow \\
\text{b. Longevity} & \longleftrightarrow & \text{d. Longevity}
\end{array}
$$

Correlation a-b is the one you get in the standard one-shot study. You can see if it is still there after the passage of time by looking at correlation c-d. To assure yourself that these are reliable measures, i.e., that you get the same answer when you do it twice, you will also look for high correlations a-c and b-d.

But the *pièce de résistance* comes when you compare correlations a-d and b-c. If Tracy Score causes Longevity, then the people with Tracy Scores in 1974 will tend to have had better retention—longevity—in 1984.

Conversely, if the main effect is that having had the paper a long time makes you a Tracy reader, the higher of the two cross-lagged correlations will be b-c. Complex path models can be built on this principle, tracing the interactions of a number of variables across time to unravel the main line of causation. This can become fairly hard to follow, but there is a simple lesson to be had from it. Causation can run both ways, but time's arrow points in only one direction. For a clean measure of a variable's presumed effect, you need to measure it *before* the effect.

The *Journal of Commerce* result was tantalizing enough to make us want to try again, this time with a true longitudinal study. The chance came in 1980 with a study of circulation retention in a town to be given here the fictitious name of Dacia.

The Leaky Bucket Model

Retention studies are based on the leaky-bucket model. The popular image is of a bucket with holes in the bottom. Water poured in at the top represents new circulation starts; to stay even you have to keep it coming in at the top at least as fast as it dribbles out the bottom. Circulation managers worry about their "churn factor," the number of new subscriptions they need to sell in a year in order to stay even, expressed as a percent of total circulation. At some newspapers, it is more than 100 percent.

The bucket is indeed leaky, but the popular picture is not quite accurate. The leaks at the bottom of the bucket are quite modest, and the readers in the bottom are stable. Most of the "churn" comes among a relatively small proportion of the circulation. So picture a bucket with most of the holes in the sides near the top. That's where the principal leaks are.

The circulation problem is to slow the churn and retard the flow out the sides of the bucket. If you keep those people in the bucket longer and continue the flow at the same rate, circulation will rise. Of course, by keeping them in, you may reduce the number available for fresh input at the top, but you can at least stabilize circulation at presumably lower cost

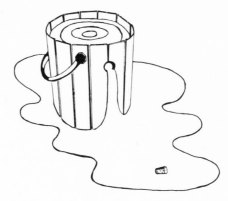

by increasing retention rather than relying on churn. So retention studies are a staple of the newspaper business.

In the Dacia study, we sought to compare the effects of the three main variables under management's control: subscription price, circulation service, and editorial quality. If their effects could be measured, it should be possible to reduce the risk in decisions to allocate resources among those three activities. A rational manager will spend the first dollar on those activities that will produce the most retention, but first he has to know what those activities are.

There are two serious problems here, one of design and one of measurement. The longitudinal design is fairly straightforward: a probability sample of some subset of subscribers. At Time 1, measure their satisfaction with price, delivery service, and editorial content. At Time 2, determine who has kept and who has dropped the paper. Construct an equation that shows the relative impact of those three variables. Change them in simulation runs to reflect hypothetical policy decisions. Compare the outcomes and the costs of those decisions to see how the most circulation can be retained for a given total cost. Because the presumed cause is being measured before the effect has occurred, there is no problem with confusing cause and effect. Nice, is it not?

What you are about to hear next is not a success story. The Dacia study cost a lot of money and never revealed as much useful information to management decision makers as it should have. But this is one of those cases where much can be learned from failure. Indeed, as Thomas Watson of IBM once advised a young writer, to succeed, you should "double your rate of failure," because it is in the failures that learning takes place (Berg, 1970). If researchers would share their failures as eagerly as their successes, the road to newspaper survival might be made a good deal shorter.

Design of the Dacia Study

A key problem in the design of this study was finding the optimum time frame. Because the effects being measured may be very slow and cumulative, the general rule would be that the more time they have to do their work, the better. However, a very long delay means problems in managing the study. The people measured in Time 1 are more likely to have drifted away if Time 2 is set too far in the future. And intervening changes in the market environment are more likely to develop to the point where they can confound the results. The other aspect of timing is that you want to finish the project and give your managers some answers while they are still interested in the problem.

The time problem is related to the other key problem, which is getting the variables to vary. Don't laugh. If everybody has the same attitude toward circulation service, price, and editorial content, there won't be anything to correlate. Regression models, remember, are based on covariance, so you have to have variance. The same is true of the dependent variable. If everybody keeps the paper or if nobody keeps it, you have no variance to measure. So the operationalization—the selection of the measures you use—has to tap these elements in the ranges where they are likely to vary.

The problem, then, was to find a way to measure variance in retention in a reasonably short period of time. And the only way to do that was to focus on groups with higher-than-normal variance, or high-risk groups. Who are the subscribers most likely to drop? The ones who most recently started. Think of the potential newspaper audience as being divided into three groups:

1. Hard-core nonreaders
2. Churners (in-and-out)
3. Permanent readers

Those who churn at the margin between readers and nonreaders are the people we want to measure. How to find them? Simple. Study the most recent starts. The Dacia project tried in several ways, following a group of 1,065 households. They were chosen as follows:

A control group of 137 normal starts in the home county—people who called up and asked for the paper without any sales pressure.
A group of 252 households that responded to solicitation efforts in 2 outlying counties.
An experimental group of 676 households that was sampled with free papers for 6 weeks.

At the end of the 6 weeks, households in the last group were called and offered the chance to subscribe to the paper. The price depended on random assignment to 1 of 4 groups: 75% of the regular price; 100%; 125% and 150%.

A male or female head of household in each of the 1,065 households provided data through a combination of telephone interviewing and self-administered questionnaires. Topics covered included socioeconomic factors, household composition, other media usage, newspaper usage, editorial content, subject interests, and others. These data were collected after the paper had started—so the respondent could make valid judgments about the content—but before the decision to continue or drop the paper. That way, time's arrow would keep the causal direction clear.

For the 389 households who joined the ranks of readers through normal means, the dependent variable was simply the length of time they kept the paper without dropping. And the goal was to quantify the relative contributions of price, delivery service, and editorial content to that decision. That meant that each of those variables had to be operationalized. Here's how that was done:

1. *Price.*   Four different price questions were scattered through the questionnaire. They took the following form: "Suppose the price of a subscription to the *Dacia Star* was $20.48 for three months. Would you subscribe for three months? That comes out to about 26 cents a copy." These questions were spaced about equally through the interview, and each time they were asked, the price came down, from the initial 150% of normal to 125%, 100%, and 75%. A household was classed

as sensitive to price if it indicated a purchase intent at one of the lower prices but not at a higher price.

2. *Delivery Service.* This was measured with a series of questions, from the very general to the very specific. The most general was, "How do you rate the home delivery service of the *Dacia Star?* Would you say it is excellent, very good, good, fair, or poor?"

Specific questions dealt with delivery time, both actual and preferred, and the incidence of problems. The latter was measured with this question: "We are interested in the quality of delivery service. Please write in how many times in the past four weeks the *Star* has: not been delivered at all; been delivered later than you wanted; been delivered in poor condition; been hard to find because of where it was put."

3. *Content.* Respondents were shown a long list of standing features—59 in the case of the *Dacia Star*—and asked to rate each on a 5-point scale where 5 stood for "I like it a lot," 1 for like it "not at all," and 0 for never reading it. Segments of the features were clipped and included in the questionnaire so the respondent would remember what he or she was grading.

The Outcome in Dacia

A number of interesting things happened. The questions about purchase interest under varying prices produced a nice distribution with plenty of variance. For the *Star,* the percent who said they would buy the paper for each price was as follows:

Price	Purchase Intent
150%	12%
125	18
100	28
75	43

The correlation is obvious to the naked eye. It works out to a correlation coefficient of .981, meaning that price explains 96% of the variance in purchase intent. And the regression equation is $Y = 71.6 - .412X$, meaning that demand is indeed elastic and drops .4% for each 1% increment of price increase.

If we had stopped right there, we would have had a lot to cheer about. Newspaper publishers are usually extremely cautious about price changes because they never know what to expect. Knowing the elasticity can be a great help in making pricing decisions. But our cheers at getting that equation, would, it turns out, have been misguided. The relevant behavior, remember, is not what people say they will do, but what they actually do, and we were in a position to measure that, too. So we did.

These questions were asked in the middle of the 6-week sampling period. At the end of the sampling period, the participants were called and given the following pitch: "I understand you have been participating in our Newspaper Research Project for the past 6 weeks, and we hope you've enjoyed getting the paper. I know when you agreed to participate in the project, we told you there would be no selling involved, but within the next couple of days we will be stopping home delivery of your *Star*. We would like to know if you want to continue delivery of your *Star* at $13.65 for the next 7 weeks. Would that be all right with you?"

The pitch was made in four randomized variations to reflect the pricing alternatives used in the original questionnaire. And the elasticity disappeared. In fact, nearly as many people agreed to buy the news at the highest price as at the lowest price. As might be expected, fewer actually agreed to buy than had said they would buy at each given price. Worse yet, when it came time to pay, very few paid for their subscriptions— regardless of the price. Here's how the proportion of the total who accepted the offer and paid for it varied by price:

Price	Paid
150%	9%
125	1
100	4
75	4

So is demand really inelastic, or is something wrong with the research? From historical records of price changes in various markets, we know that demand really is price-elastic. And the .4% drop for each 1% increase in price first found in the survey is consistent with that historical experience. That leads to a suspicion that something was wrong with the experiment. At least 2 possibilities come to mind:

1. Dacia was a very high-penetration newspaper market to start with. The people in the experiment, because of the way they were

selected, came more from the hard-core nonreader group than the target churn group. Hard-core nonreaders tend to be poor and uneducated with the newspaper very low on their list of needs. When it came to actually getting members of this group to subscribe to the paper *and* pay for it, there was not enough variance to get a good measurement.

2. The sales pitch masked the price difference. The $13.65 price was cited in all 4 sales pitches with the variance coming in the number of weeks that amount could buy. It ranged from 16 weeks for the condition with 75% of normal price to 7 weeks for the high-price condition. To unsophisticated consumers, the 7-week offer may have seemed like less of a commitment and therefore more attractive. Holding subscription length constant and varying the dollar amount might have worked better.

Why vary the time instead of the dollar value? We knew better. But the circulation department was afraid that respondents would compare notes, discover the price differences, and become confused or angry. We should have fought harder for a pure price comparison.

We were still left with a measure of price sensitivity that looked good on paper to use with the group of respondents who had acquired the paper through normal means and were therefore more likely to be part of the churn. But we were so discouraged by the gap between stated intent and behavior in the experimental group that we were reluctant to make any generalizations from it. So much for the effort to link price to circulation retention.

That left circulation service and editorial content. Circulation service turned out to be another kind of disaster—not because it was bad but because it was so good. None of the questions that we thought were such ingenious measures was able to pick up any variance. Nearly everybody loved the service, gave it the highest ratings, couldn't remember any cases of late, wet, or missing papers. What could we have done differently? Two things:

1. We might have loaded the questions to make it easier to criticize the circulation service. This was not an attempt to get a vote of confidence in the circulation department, but to uncover the vari-

ance in service satisfaction. What we did was like trying to measure oven temperature with a freezer thermometer. The variance, if any, was off our scale.
2. We could have concentrated on geographic areas of known circulation problems—outlying areas with recently inaugurated home delivery service, for example.

The Editorial Variable

That left one of the three variables to use in predicting retention: the respondent's evaluation of the editorial content. This one worked. The variance was beautiful. And we found a number of ways to use it.

One was a simple count of the number of features read and given a high rating. The greater that number, the longer the retention. There are very few occasions in newspaper research when you can demonstrate a causal relationship between editorial content and retention. This was one.

Perhaps the reason this part of the project worked so well was that we had done it before. Ed Mumford of the *Philadelphia Inquirer* had worked out the system of combining telephone and mail interviewing. An interviewer makes the first contact by telephone, asks whatever screening questions are needed to establish the respondent's eligibility, and then obtains the respondent's agreement to participate. Those who agree receive a package in the mail.

In one version of this method, the package is simply a booklet of exhibits—sample clippings from the newspaper. After allowing time for it to arrive, the interviewer calls again, guides the respondent through the booklet, and asks about the various features displayed there. In a cheaper version, the booklet is an illustrated, self-administered questionnaire.

Because this method produces a scaled evaluation of each feature, as well as a count of which ones are read, it can be used in a great variety of regression-based techniques, including factor analysis. The use of factor analysis to attack the comic strip problem to be described in Chapter 9 can also be applied to the whole range of newspaper features. By learning the clustered patterns of reading, an editor can make better judgments about which areas to enhance and even how to lay out the paper. In one market, for example, an editorial-page columnist was clustered, not with other editorial-page features, but with folksy, down-to-earth kinds of content—a signal that he belonged in the local section rather than on the editorial page. And the referendum—the basic number of readers a feature has—makes more sense when a feature's popularity is compared with others in its factor group rather than with the total content of the paper.

And if total number of features read can be shown to predict retention, it may be possible to design and analyze a study that shows the relative contribution of different classes of features or even individual features to retention. The problem is not intractable, but, because it cannot be solved without considerable trial and error, it needs some more risky experimentation. We all need to increase our rate of failure if we are to expand our research horizons.

We all love psychographics. They make it possible to reduce large and complex populations to a few simple types that imagination can see as flesh-and-blood personalities instead of numerical abstractions. The fact that these reductions are gross oversimplifications is not really a disadvantage. Everyone who markets consumer products keeps a picture in his or her head of the person who will be using those products.

For my high-school journalism teacher, that mythical target was a twelve-year-old child. If the child could understand what was in the newspaper, she told us, most other people could too. Edwin A. Lahey advised his correspondents in Washington to "write for people who move their lips when they read." And there was the Omaha milkman, immortalized by a United Press correspondent named William Shepherd who wrote a widely admired account of a factory fire in New York in 1911 and explained, "I just write for the milkman in Omaha. I figure if he can understand what I am writing, then everybody can understand it."

In today's marketing environment, however, a single customer stereotype is no longer sufficient. Marketers follow a strategy of segmentation that calls for them to simultaneously appeal to many different kinds of customers, each looking for different kinds of value.

There is, however, a limit to the mind's ability to maintain an image of a very large number of market segments. Some reduction of data is necessary. Marketers need a concept that is simpler than the vast array of potential segments but more complicated than the Omaha milkman. Psychographic classification of the audience offers some hope of providing such a workable concept.

There are many different ways to perform statistical classifications, and there is even a periodical, *The Journal of Classification*, edited at the University of Illinois, where specialists in this exotic field share their methods and their discoveries. One psychographic classification system, created by the non-profit SRI International, of Menlo Park, California, has gained particular notice because of its use in a great variety of marketing problems. Called VALS, for values and life styles, it divides consumers in the United States into nine basic types which a marketing specialist can picture in his or her head. The appeal is in the visualization, and many other market researchers have been inspired to try their own classification schemes.

Clusters vs. Factors

Most psychographic studies are anything but simple. The availability of high-powered computer techniques and elegant mathematical models tempts researchers to squeeze more apparent meaning from survey data than may be justified by the data's validity. Moreover, the classification techniques frequently used often produce solutions that are too unstable to permit comparisons across time or across markets. Factor analysis, a data reduction tool, has been abused by analysts who confuse factors with clusters (Stewart, 1981). In psychographic applications, clusters are groups of people with similar characteristics, while factors are groups of attributes that tend to apply to the same people. One might, for example, conduct both kinds of analyses on a population of real and imaginary adventurers in literature. A cluster analysis might show the following to be members of the same cluster:

> Lawrence of Arabia
> Robinson Crusoe
> Coronado
> Don Quixote

An R-type factor analysis, on the other hand, might tell us that certain attributes go together:

> hot
> dusty
> sunburned
> thirsty

It is the same data looked at in different ways. R-type factor analysis is generally easier to use. Some of the most common computer statistical packages have it, and there are well-established rules for the definition of factors. The most popular applications produce factors that are not highly correlated with one another, a lack that helps to reassure the researcher that each factor is measuring a different underlying attribute. But because the factors are uncorrelated, sorting people into mutually exclusive categories based on each person's degree of identification with the different factors requires another step. To treat the factor clusters is like saying a person is fatter than he is smart. Such statements are usually not very helpful (but see the comic-strip example in chapter 9 for an interesting exception).

A Simpler Way

Valid classification schemes can be created in a number of ways, some of them quite intricate. One is to use the dimensions identified in a factor analysis as variables in a cluster analysis—a technique which has hundreds of variants. Another is to use the factors to create scales along more than one dimension. This chapter outlines a very simple way of doing the latter. This simple method will not be universally applicable, but it can serve to illustrate the logic behind a classification scheme. It was used in a series of projects for various newspapers in the Knight-Ridder group, whose cities will be identified in this chapter with the fictitious names Avalon, Barbary, and Cipango. It is the result of an effort to find a psychographic classification scheme that is simple and meets three other tests:

1. The measurement should be objective enough to be replicable for comparisons across time and across markets.
2. The definitions should be intuitively sensible.
3. The categories should discriminate between readers of different newspapers.

The project began with secondary analysis of data collected by a research supplier among newspaper readers in Avalon. Respondents told interviewers whether they agreed strongly, agreed, disagreed, or disagreed strongly to each of 84 statements provided by the supplier. Readers unfamiliar with this sort of inquiry can get the flavor of such items from Daniel M. Wegner's "Hidden Brain-Damage Scale" described in *American Psychologist* (1979):

1. I never liked room temperature.
2. Pudding without raisins is no pudding at all.
3. Walls impede my progress.
4. Armenians are comical in full-battle dress.

While Wegner and his friends claimed to have been kidding, the items used in serious psychographic research sometimes have the same mad ring. The 84 variables in the Avalon study were reduced in the reanalysis to five factors using one of the prepackaged computer programs. As it almost always does, the program produced several factors that seemed plausible, each factor defined by a list of variables selected from the original 84. Variables in each list correlated in varying degree with the underlying dimension or factor. In this case, there were five factors that made sense, which was a relief, because five are much easier to deal with than 84.

This is the point at which it is healthy to deprive factor analysis of some of its mystique. The five factors can be treated simply as scales. Scaling is something researchers do when more precision is needed than is available from a single survey question. By asking several questions on the same subject, we increase the probability that we are measuring what we think we are measuring. These questions form scales, and the skeptical investigator can verify that all the items in a scale measure approximately the same thing by ascertaining that the items are intercorrelated, i.e., a respondent's answer to one of the items is likely to be consistent with his or her answers on the others.

Factor analysis, as applied here, is nothing more than a quick method of finding scales. The computer sorts individual questionnaire items into groups, each group measures approximately the same thing, and the groups are listed neatly. To make things even neater, we give these lists names and treat them as variables. In choosing the names, we are about as scientific as little girls naming their dolls, but it does help us keep track of them.

Choosing Factors That Discriminate

The next step was to see which, if any, factors discriminated between readers of different newspapers in the Avalon market. To make the distinction clear-cut, newspaper readers were divided into three mutually exclusive groups according to the newspaper that each individual read the most. Those who read two papers equally were left out of this part of the analysis.

A mean factor score was then calculated for each of the readership groups. A factor score, for this purpose, is simply an index number that tells how stongly each respondent in the survey is associated with the attitudes represented by a given factor. Technically, it is a correlation coefficient, and so it has a range of 1 to −1.

Table 5 shows how the average reader of each newspaper scored on each factor. We were particularly interested in factors that would discriminate between readers of Paper A and Paper C. The factors that performed this service most effectively were Modernism and Traditionalism.

At this point, because we had long-range applications of the methods in mind, we asked ourselves whether it was really necessary to burden respondents with 84 different agree-disagree questions to produce this result. We therefore isolated the five variables with the strongest association with each of the five factors and discarded the rest, thus narrowing Urban's original list of 84 variables to 25.

When the shortened list was run through the factor analysis program, the same factors emerged neatly arrayed with each of the five variables belonging to the same factor with which it had been associated before. And, once again, the Modernism and Traditionalism factors proved to be the best discriminators between readers of Paper A and Paper C (Table 6). As a further check, correlation coefficients were calculated between the long- and short-form factor scores. There was high correlation (Table 7). This knowledge would enable us to cut respondent burden and field costs when we took the procedure to Barbary and Cipango.

Defining Reader Types

Now that we know that Modernism and Traditionalism help to identify the readers of different newspapers, it is time to look at the substance of these indicators. The statements that define Modernism deal with contemporary behavior:

Modernism

1. There are situations where sex outside of marriage can be a healthy thing.
2. I like to think I'm a bit of a swinger.

TABLE 5

Mean Factor Scores for Readership Groups

Version 1—with 84 variables

	A	B	C
Modernism 1	−.0228	.2961	−.0639
Traditionalism 1	.0504	.2078	−.1164
Losing 1	−.0898	.2128	−.0920
Coping 1	.0202	−.0386	.0379
Cosmopolitanism 1	.1138	−.3289	.1128

TABLE 6

Mean Factor Scores for Readership Groups

Version 2—with 25 variables

	A	B	C
Modernism 2	−.0075	.2481	−.0688
Traditionalism 2	.0746	.0293	−.0599
Losing 2	−.0829	.1598	−.0682
Coping 2	−.0383	.0285	.0028
Cosmopolitanism 2	.0780	−.2675	.0903

TABLE 7

Correlations between Original Factor Scores
and Short Factor Scores

Modernism	.862
Traditionalism	.784
Losing	.803
Coping	.775
Cosmopolitanism	.885

3. I would like to live in a foreign city, like Paris, for a year.
4. Sometimes I say or do things just to shock people.
5. I'm really basically a "night" person.

The statements that define Traditionalism deal with nostalgia and traditional roles for women:

Traditionalism

1. I often wish for the good old days when life was simpler.
2. Young people have too much freedom today.
3. There is too much emphasis on sex today.

4. A woman's place is in the home.
5. Women's lib has gone too far.

Now we can classify each respondent as high or low on each of the 2 factors, choosing cutting points that will yield categories of equal size. For the sake of further simplicity, these scores are obtained by simple arithmetic. Strong agreement is given the value of 4, agreement 3, disagreement 2, and strong disagreement 1. By averaging each respondent's score for each question, we get a range of values from 1 to 4. (Where data are missing, the respondent is scored according to his average on the values present.)

We do this at a certain cost. Instead of using a simple numeric average, we could let the factor scores represent each person's position on each scale—just as we did earlier when we compared the factors based on 84 variables to those based on only 25. If we did this, the complete noncorrelation of the factors would be assured. The procedure makes them come out that way. In using the simple average instead, there is a risk that there will be some correlation between the two.

This is a small price to pay for what we get in return, which is a pair of scales that is easy to understand. We never lose our intuitive feeling for what it takes to be high or low. To set a standard scale that will be applied to other samples, a certain amount of arbitrariness is necessary anyway, and there is no great harm in simplifying this way. To think otherwise would be to treat the sample survey, on which these data are based, as a more delicate instrument than it really is. And our reward for this modesty is what social scientists call "face validity," meaning that the scales can be taken to mean pretty much what they appear to mean.

The cutting points in Avalon (later applied to other cities when we wanted to make cross-market comparisons) define scores of 2 or less as low for Modernism and 2.6 or less as low for Traditionalism. These divisions produced 4 categories:

1. High Modernism, high Traditionalism
2. High Modernism, low Traditionalism
3. Low Modernism, low Traditionalism
4. Low Modernism, high Traditionalism

Do these categories make intuitive sense? By considering the substantive meaning of the individual items in the 2 scales we can try to discern the meaning of the categories and even give them names.

People in the first group, high Modernism and high Traditionalism, appear to be living in conflict. They want adventures, like living in a foreign city or doing things to shock people, but they also wish for the good old days when life was simpler. They give qualified approval to sex outside of marriage, yet believe there is too much emphasis on sex today. They seem to be trying to find themselves. Let's call them "Seekers."

The second group, high Modernism and low Traditionalism, is more consistent. Its members are forward-looking, adventurous, negative toward the old values while adopting the new, and ready to take risks. Label them "Adventurers."

In the third group, low Modernism with low Traditionalism, we find people free of the older values and yet too cautious to be tempted by the unconventional or risky. Perhaps they are ready to move forward, but they are careful; they appear to be quiet, unspectacular achievers. Tag them "Watchers."

Finally, we have those low in Moderenism and high in Traditionalism. These people are the consistent, opposite number of the Adventurers. They don't want to take chances, do things differently, or cope with modern life. They are bothered by sex, women's lib, and the freedom of young people. They must worry a lot. And so they are the "Worriers."

We thus have 2 dimensions defining 4 mutually exclusive categories. If the 2 dimensions were completely uncorrelated, we would expect the number of people in each of the 4 cells to be about the same. Because there is slight negative correlation, the cells defined by conflict in attitudes are somewhat smaller. Here is the distribution in Avalon in 1977:

Seekers	16%
Adventurers	33
Worriers	31
Watchers	20
	100

Every person in the survey can be placed in a 2-dimensional space denoting a position on each scale. That space becomes a kind of psychological map. More importantly, we can average the values on the two scales for the readers of each of the 3 newspapers and compare the positions of those averages in that space. By finding out what kind of people

FIGURE 7

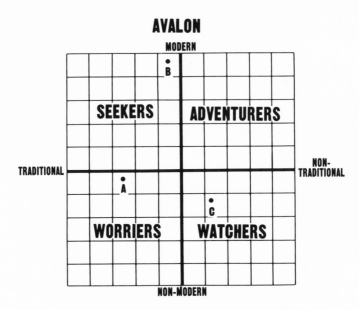

its customers are, a marketer can learn what kind of a product he or she has.

In Avalon, the average reader of each of the newspapers fell into a different quadrant (Figure 7). For the strategic planner, the empty space where the Adventurers are defined may represent a marketing opportunity. None of the three papers had clearly established a predominant appeal to that audience.

Is this audience worth appealing to? Examination of the demographics of the four groups suggests that it is.

In Avalon, the Adventurers were found most frequently in the 18 to 34 age group. They were high in education and tended to be professionals, executives, or students. They had more than their proportionate share of single people, and incomes were high. Many came from households of more than one wage earner.

From other research we know that this is the group that accounts for much of the loss in newspaper readership since the late 1960s. An editor whose typical readers are found in the other three quadrants might well consider how to change the product's image to appeal to this group.

The other categories also had distinctive demographics. Seekers tended to come from the young-middle-aged groups, persons who had not graduated from college, skilled workers and craftsmen, and low-to-middle income households. They included a disproportionate number of single males.

Worriers came from the older age brackets and lower education groups. Homemakers were over-represented, as were Catholics and Protestants. They were more likely to be widowed or divorced. Incomes were low with a disproportionate share of one-person households and unemployed persons.

The Watchers were mainly young-middle-aged and older and came from all but the very lowest educational attainment levels. They had a somewhat disproportionate share of homemakers and other married females.

As an additional check on the simplified form of data collection for the factor analysis, demographics were checked against members of the four quadrants when the long form (84 variables) of the input to the factor analysis was used. The long form produced somewhat sharper distinctions, but the main demographic differences held constant.

So far, this psychographic description of the Avalon newspaper market appears to meet two of the three tests we set out to meet. The definitions are intuitively satisfying, and they do discriminate among readers of different newspapers.

But are they transferable to other markets? To effect such a transfer, we need two things. One is some reassurance that the same items, factor analyzed from samples of other populations, will continue to produce the same factors. The other is that the categories have simple operational definitions that do not depend on the peculiarities of a given market.

The latter test is easily met by using the standardized cutting points. But for the former test, we must repeat the factor analysis in each new market. This was done. The reduced list of 25 lifestyle items was asked about in a survey of the adult population of Barbary in 1979. When these items were factor analyzed, the Modernism and Traditionalism factors emerged with clarity equal to that found in Avalon.

Thus encouraged, we discarded all of the items from the original list

TABLE 8

Average Scores in the Three Markets

	Avalon	Barbary	Cipango
Modernism	2.12	2.21	1.93
Traditionalism	2.71	2.60	2.55

except for the bare minimum of ten needed to define Traditionalists and Moderns. To enrich the stew, we added some other items of particular interest to the Cipango market and ran a survey there in 1980. Once again, the five Modernism items clustered on the same factor, and the five Traditionalism items clustered on another factor, verifying yet again the internal consistency of each scale. The average scale values are shown for each market in Table 8.

Barbary ranked significantly higher in Modernism and lower in Traditionalism than Avalon, while Cipango was lower on both dimensions than either of the other two cities. These differences are not inconsistent with what is otherwise known about geographic and cultural differences among the three locations. When Barbary and Cipango residents are classified according to each city's own mean, a psychological map can be plotted for each city to give some guidance to editors and strategic planners (Figures 8 and 9). The Barbary map shows two morning newspapers (A and B) in the Adventurer quadrant and two afternoon papers (C and D) in the Worrier quadrant. Because papers A and C were produced by the same people in the belief that they were serving the same audience, this finding was considerably enlightening to the editors. The fact that paper A was also quite close on the map to its rival, paper B, had some significance for strategists who had been considering how best to position it for the competitive battle.

In the case of Cipango, papers A and B, under one ownership, are shown to be quite centrist in their appeal, as contrasted to C and D, under a different ownership, which appealed to more distinctive segments. In every case, the strategic implications are fairly straightforward. The reliability of the method is affirmed by the fact that the four psychographic groups are associated with the same demographics in each of the three markets. Adventurers are consistently the young, upwardly mobile, working people. Watchers are always older and more conservative. Seekers tend to be lower-income, less educated, working people. And Worriers are aging, downscale, and disproportionately female.

FIGURE 8

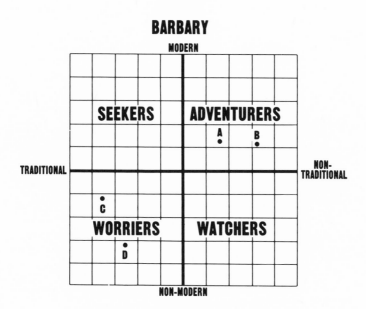

If this is so, why not analyze the audience by demographics alone? Leo Bogart has warned in *American Psychologist* that attempts to classify market segments by psychological characteristics "often end up merely as restatements of age or social class differences." However, the psychographic restatements are far more interesting and appealing to decision makers. A marketing planner can take the test and calculate his or her own Modernism and Traditionalism scores and find a self-image on the psychological map. Awareness of the distance between the marketer and his or her customers on that map is made easy by the map's graphic power. That power can even be used to visualize statistical significance. The points denoting means on the map can be surrounded by circles or ellipses showing the range of the standard error. In Cipango, for example, the circles for A and B would nearly touch, indicating a difference of low significance.

The self-administered form of the test has never failed to provoke lively discussion at management seminars, and one newspaper researcher I know has even taken to using it as a conversation stimulator in singles bars. Any device researchers can employ to gain the attentive interest of their clients is worth using so long as it carries a payload of useful information.

The method described here is designed to give stability to a slippery concept. But in the long run, very little may be stable in classification research. The scales described here worked well enough in three cities, but failed in a fourth. In 1981, in a place quite different in size and geography from the first three, the scales fell apart. The items did not hang together as neatly and did not fall into the same pattern in the factor analysis. The difference could have been in time, geography, or methodology. Fortunately, enough new question items, dealing with matters that seemed relevant to that time and place, had been included so that a new classification scheme could be created from scratch—something the prudent researcher should be prepared to do.

The relative simplicity of the method also has the advantage of removing it from some of the esoteric quibbles that often surround factor analy-

FIGURE 9

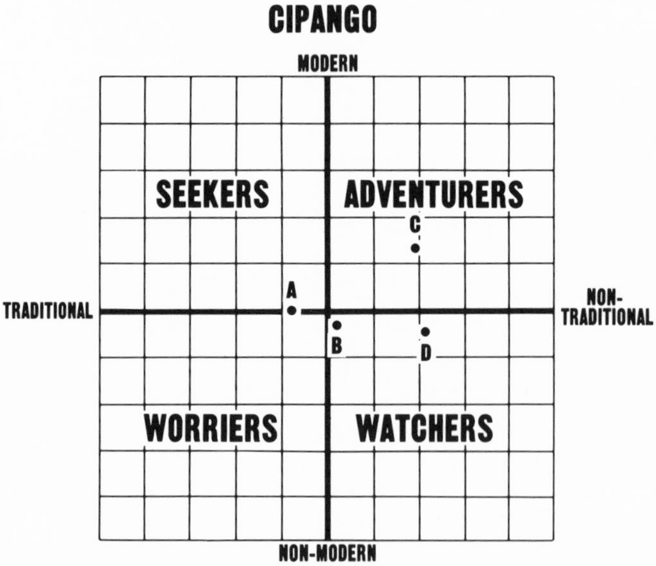

sis. The kind of factor rotation used and the number of factors extracted are not too important. The factor analysis is used only as an interim step to lead to some scales that will discriminate among users of different products. Once we have found those scales, we needn't be too concerned about how we got them so long as their internal consistency is maintained. That consistency can be checked by repeated factor analysis in other populations or simply by inspection of the correlation matrix. If all of the items in a scale intercorrelate, they are probably measuring the same thing, and the scale is probably a reliable measure of that thing, whatever it is. Modernism and Traditionalism and the groups that they define were real in at least three cities. And this form of simplified psychographics has promise for the discovery of other dimensions that may shed light on the characteristics of a newspaper's market.

Appendix: Self Test

This is a model that makes more sense if you can find yourself in it. Here's how. Below are five statements. For each one, indicate whether you agree strongly, agree, disagree, or disagree strongly.

	AS	A	D	DS
1. I'm really basically a "night" person.	4	3	2	1
2. Sometimes I do or say things to shock people	4	3	2	1
3. I would like to live in a foreign city, like Paris, for a year.	4	3	2	1
4. I like to think I'm a bit of a swinger.	4	3	2	1
5. There are situations where sex outside of marriage can be a healthy thing.	4	3	2	1

Total your scores to the above five questions. This is your *modernism* score. Now go on to the next five questions.

1. I often wish for the good old days when life was simpler.	4	3	2	1
2. A woman's place is in the home.	4	3	2	1
3. Young people have too much freedom today.	4	3	2	1
4. Women's lib has gone too far.	4	3	2	1
5. There is too much emphasis on sex today.	4	3	2	1

Total these in the same way. This is your *traditionalism* score. Use your scores to decide in which of the two Modernism rows and the two Traditionalism columns your answers place you.

	Traditionalism	
	0–13	14–20
Modernism 0–10	Watcher	Worrier
Modernism 11–20	Adventurer	Seeker

Now find your group's profile below and see if it fits you.

Seeker

You are forward-looking and adventurous but nevertheless careful to maintain your respect for traditional values. These impulses sometimes conflict, causing stress of the sort described by Alvin Toffler in *Future Shock.* Chances are you are in early middle age (late 30s to 40s) and have achieved higher job status than most people of your educational attainment. If a racy tabloid is published where you live, you probably read it.

Worrier

The world moves too fast for you. You are acutely aware of social change and usually unhappy about it. Both social innovaiton and personal risk-taking are unpleasant for you. You are probably in late middle age or beyond, and your income and education are below average. You have lived most of your life in one place, and your reading habits resemble those of your parents.

Watcher

You are educated, responsible, and careful. You face the future with confidence, knowing that your natural inclination is to avoid unnecessary risks. Your age could be anywhere from late youth to incipient retirement. You tend to be tolerant of those who move at a more reckless pace while inching steadily toward your own goals. You want hard news in your newspaper.

Adventurer

You are young, well-educated, and venturesome. If not still in college, you have embarked on a career as an executive or professional. Chances are that you have more discretionary income than most people your age. You are either single or have a working spouse. Your information needs are eclectic.

Running Your Own / 8.
Focus Group

Of all the methods for gathering data about newspaper readers, the focus group can often provide the most intuitive satisfaction. The information comes from flesh and blood people without being processed through coders, interviewers, and computers. An editor can size them up directly and even question them himself. The method is also flexible. It is not guided by an automatic, rigid schedule of questions. Instead, an interviewer can follow and develop new ideas as they turn up.

Another advantage of this type of research is that it is fast and cheap. A focus group can be assembled on a few days' notice, and the cash outlay can be limited to the small stipend paid to participants. Therefore, it is not surprising that an increasing number of editors have expressed interest in running their own focus groups. This chapter tells how to do it.

What Focus Groups Are Good For

The focus group is primarily an idea-generating device, a preliminary form of research. You can think of it as the analog of a library search. Before an investigative reporter sets out on a project, he first combs the clip file to see what else has been written on the subject and what clues and ideas might be turned up. In a focus group you search the minds of your participants for ideas, clues, and approaches that might not have occurred to you if you were simply sitting in a room by yourself. Some of the ideas generated will have value that is considerable on its face. Others will be intriguing but clearly need further testing before they are acted on. Still others will be useless. And a good many will be ambiguous. The point is to dredge up as much material of all types as you can, sort it out, and then go on from there.

And you have to go on. The preliminary nature of this kind of research should never be forgotten. When it leads to new ideas on which you might base some action, you will usually want to follow up with hard, quantitative research to back up the impressionistic data you have gleaned from the focus group.

What Focus Groups Are Not Good For

You can't generalize from a focus group. No group of eight to ten people is representative of your community or your readership at large unless the characteristic you are measuring is something that exists uniformly throughout the population. There are such traits: body temperature, give or take a few tenths of a degree; or number of fingers or toes. But the things we are usually interested in investigating interest us precisely because they are variable, and therefore we need to sample in a sophisticated manner in order to generalize. No one has yet devised a way of making a focus group representative of anything, and so findings must always be interpreted with caution and a conscious disavowal of intent to generalize.

Even when the disclaimer is made, it is easy to forget. The output from a focus group can be so interesting that you may find yourself saying, "Of course we can't generalize from this . . ." and then proceeding to spend the next hour generalizing from it. Always remember that the purpose of focus group interviews is to generate ideas and hypotheses for further testing, not to produce research "findings."

Defining the Problem

A focus group is a limited tool best applied to limited goals. You may feel like sitting down with a group of readers and saying, "Just tell me all about your attitudes toward the newspaper." But you can't! You need to focus on a specific problem dealing with a limited segment of your audience. If you want to study a lot of problems among a number of segments, you will simply have to form a lot of focus groups.

Here are some examples of limited topics and special audiences:

Readership of the sports pages by blacks.
Use of the Lifestyle section by working women.
Children's use of parts of the newspaper directed at them.
How business and professional men view the editorial page.

The Discussion Outline

Once the general research question has been defined, it should be broken up into its component parts. William D. Wells (1974), writing on group interviewing in the *Handbook of Marketing Research,* recommends preparing a list of questions that you expect this research project to answer. This list is not necessarily the list of questions that will be put to the respondents. The interview won't be that structured. But it helps to have a little checklist of things that you hope to find out so that as you go through the interview you can make sure that the bases are all being covered. For example:

What do newspaper readers think about the people who produce the newspaper? Do they regard them as personalities or as faceless entities? Does the newspaper itself have a personality? If so, is it uniform across all parts of the paper, or does it vary from one section to another? How do readers decide what to read? In what order do they tackle different parts of the paper, and at what time of the day? Do they use the newspaper more for general knowledge or for specific facts that they need to make it through the day? Do they ever remember bylines? If so, what bylines can they remember? Is the relationship between reader and newspaper warm and human or cold and impersonal?

One reason for having such a detailed set of questions is that it lets you reassure yourself that you have thought about what you hope to find out. It also ensures that everyone on the staff who is participating on this project has had a voice and has participated in reaching agreement on the specific objectives. This is especially important in a focus group interview as compared with other kinds of research projects because it provides just about the only structure that the interview is going to have.

You can work from this question list, or, as Wells suggests, you can write a simple topic outline to be used to guide the interview. The actual questions that are put to respondents will depend very much on how the flow of the interview goes, and you want to keep it loose enough so that questions can be framed to fit that flow. The topic outline keeps you from straying too far afield and reminds you to keep things on the track sufficiently so that all of the research points are covered.

Choosing the Interviewer

Some researchers think it is unwise for editors to do their own focus group interviewing. The theory is that editors have a vested interest in the answers, and a more neutral interviewer might elicit better responses. My own view is that it depends on the editor. Someone who can detach himself or herself from the topic and probe for information in a friendly and dispassionate manner will make a good interviewer regardless of his or her regular occupation.

It is also a good idea to look around the other departments of the newspaper for people who are good at relating to others and drawing them out. People in the personnel deparment who have had academic training in psychology might be available. Also consider the promotion deparment, where you are likely to have someone who meets people easily and would make a good facilitator.

If you do decide to hire a professional, the cost will not be very great compared to that of other research projects. You can save money by forgoing a written report or by writing the report yourself.

Recruiting

Novices at group interviewing tend to try for too much diversity in the group. Getting lots of different kinds of people in the hope of producing a lot of different kinds of ideas sounds logical, but it doesn't bear up in practice. If the people are too different from one another they will be ill at ease and find it difficult to communicate. You need people who have enough experiences in common to form the basis for good communication.

Wells says that uniformity is especially important with respect to social class and stage in the family life cycle. Young people are likely to defer to those who are older and more experienced and the presence of literate and articulate middle-class respondents will inhibit participation by downscale interviewees.

You should, therefore, set rigid demographic requirements for your group, for example:

Business and professional men over 45.
Working women with young children.
College students.
Blue-collar football fans.

The best way to recruit is to go through the telephone book, calling people at random, and administering a structured interview that screens for the desired characteristics. A person who passes all of the screening tests is then invited to the interview. For a sample screening interview, see the end of this chapter.

How large should the group be? First, size up the physical accommodations. Count the number of chairs that will fit around a table. A group smaller than six will usually not produce enough interaction. Groups larger than ten can be a bit unwieldy and do not allow for enough participation by each person. One or two will usually have last minute problems in getting babysitters or tending to other personal business and will fail to show up, so you need to over-recruit.

Some researchers say that different members of the same family or friends should not attend the same group. The theory is that this will make the group too homogeneous or that people will be less candid in the presence of their friends or relatives. Other researchers, however, think that having friends and relatives produces more naturalness and makes the conversation go easier. In fact, some groups intentionally are composed of family members, as when couples are invited to discuss the kinds of purchases that usually require joint agreement. On the whole, the advantages and disadvantages of allowing friends and relatives to participate in the same group may balance out, but it will depend on the subject matter.

Be sure that you are recruiting virgin respondents. If you are recruiting through channels that have been used before for this purpose, such as a civic organization or even a research firm, you may get people who have done this before. Focus group participation is enjoyable, and many people who do it once are eager to come back for more. Some are so eager that they may figure out the right answers in the screening interview and give false information so that they can be included. And professional field services have been known to throw in their own interviewers to fill a respondent chair at the last minute. Don't let them get away with that. You want freshness and innocence in the ideas that are generated. Too much time spent in focus groups makes a respondent jaded and overly sophisticated in a way that can lead you down a wrong path.

Where to Hold the Interview

A conference room with a long table and just the right number of chairs is ideal, but it is not a necessity. You can hold a focus group in someone's living room. The friendly, familiar setting helps people relax, but there are some disadvantages. Most people will know where the newspaper office is, but a private residence can be hard to find. And there are more likely to be distractions. The telephone rings. Or the hostess has to leave to answer the door or to let out the cat from time to time.

Some marketing research firms will rent special rooms designed for focus groups with hidden recorders, video equipment, and one-way glass for observers to sit behind. Some will try to convince you that you can't have a focus group without one-way glass. Don't believe them.

The one-way glass is for the benefit of the observers, not to make the participants feel more comfortable. It enables the observers to make tasteless jokes, talk on the telephone, eat and drink, nap, or do other things that would be considered antisocial in the direct presence of the interviewees. There is nothing wrong with having well-behaved observers sit in the same room with the interviewees. Keep them off to one side of the room and acknowledge their presence, then ask the group to ignore them. A well-run group will quickly forget about the audience as it gets into the subject matter of the discussion. Sometime during the second half of the interview you can invite the observers to take part and ask some of the questions themselves.

Equipment

All you really need is a tape recorder. Put it on the table in plain sight, explain what it is for, and then invite everybody to forget it. If you don't make a big deal of it, no one is likely to object.

Videotaping is a little more cumbersome, but it is useful if you want to preserve an edited-down record of the event that you can show to others. Most people have seen television commercials involving interviews with what appear to be ordinary people, and you should explain that these pictures are not being made for that purpose. Otherwise, folks may become unbearably self-conscious.

Fees

According to Ruth Clark (1979), who wrote an excellent guide to operating a focus group at the end of her widely distributed report, *Changing Needs of Changing Readers*, the going rate is $10 to $40. You pay the higher figure or even more if your group is extremely specialized. How specialized? You'll find out soon enough when you start making calls and see how many it takes to recruit one subject. A short-cut that sometimes works is to recruit your subjects through a civic group that is interested in raising some money. This helps solve the homogeneity problem, and you may get by with one flat payment to the organization.

In either case, pay the fee up front. That way, you make it clear that the fee is not contingent on what they say or how well they perform. It also places some responsibility on them. They are not used to getting paid for their opinions, and it helps to remind them that what they have to say is worth money to you.

Refreshments

Booze is out. It makes some participants argumentative and aggressive. Others go to sleep. Serve coffee, tea, soda, diet and caffeine-free drinks, and cookies at the beginning of the session. If you are dealing with genteel, upscale types, wine and cheese are acceptable.

Timing

Invite the group for 7:30 p.m. Start at 8:00 to allow for the latecomers and to give everybody time to partake of the refreshments. End at 9:30 unless everybody is having so much fun that they insist on keeping you longer.

Getting Started

Most interviewers like to call people by name, so it helps if name cards are on the table. Start by asking each person to identify himself or herself and tell a little bit about what he or she does and his or her family. This serves two purposes. It breaks the ice and gets everybody to talk at least once. And it puts some relevant information about social class and family composition on the record.

Also, it gives the interviewer a chance to show that he is interested in more than one-word responses. The interviewer should start at this point to draw out those people who reply in monosyllables or unduly brief answers. This lets everybody know right away that longer answers are okay.

Next, it's a good idea to give the situation some structure. Explain what's going on without going into an overly detailed introduction. Here are some of the points that should be made:

1. We're going to talk about the newspaper, and if you don't like the paper, they are not going to fire me. It's okay to say what's on your mind.
2. We're not here to take votes or reach a consensus. It's okay to disagree with one another. I want to hear all sides.
3. Don't be afraid to share your views with each other. It's okay for you to ask questions of each other. You don't always have to address the chair.
4. Please talk one at a time.

To get the group warmed up, you may have to ask a specific question and go around the table and ask each person to answer it in turn. This tactic may have to be used later in the interview, too, whenever it seems that participation is becoming unbalanced with 20 percent of the people doing 80 percent of the talking. There are other ways to maintain balance, of course. An alert interviewer will notice the people who seem hesitant and those who look as though they want to speak and call on them when an opportunity arises.

Keeping It Going

When the discussion is off and running, check the outline from time to time to make sure that all of the points will be covered within the time allotted. There is no need to try to take them up in any particular order. Let the order flow from the discussion. Sometimes the first issues raised are the most critical ones. An interviewer has to behave like a cat stalking a mouse, always watchful, patient, and ready to dart in this direction or that when a promising idea or even a hint of an idea surfaces.

Remember to have people talk about their needs rather than about their solutions to problems. They are not here to tell you how to edit the newspaper. They are here to tell you what is missing from their lives. Figuring out how to fill those needs is up to you.

Don't be overly self-conscious about your interviewing technique. You don't need to be a professional interviewer. You should be able to blend in with the group, participate, understand what is being said, and react in a bland, neutral way, just enough to keep the conversation going.

The Report

Sometimes no report is necessary. If all of the staff members who need to know the information generated by the group are present, you might find that no formal report is needed. Usually, however, you will want to preserve some record of the interview.

As a start, you should have the tape transcribed and edited to take out the worst of the false starts and grammatical misdirections. This will take a good secretary about one day. With the transcript in hand, writing the report is fairly easy. You want to preserve the original flavor of the interview, so long, verbatim quotes are most helpful.

Wells proposes an easy method for organizing the report. Go through the transcript and mark with numbers and brackets those quotes that illustrate the chief themes. Then take scissors and cut the transcript up so that all of the quotes pertaining to each theme are together. All you need to do then is write some interpretation and exposition to connect the verbatim portions. If you are handy with a word processor, you won't need scissors.

In writing the report, keep in mind the fact that the statements made in group interviews are not generalizable to larger populations.

How Many Interviews?

If the subject is worth discussing in one focus group, it is worth doing twice. The typical pattern is that in the first group interview, you get a lot of fresh ideas and interesting insights. In the second group interview, you get some repetition of what you learned in the first, but a good deal more than that, which because of natural human diversity never surfaced at all the first time. You need the second interview, then, to guard against the possibility that some extremely valuable idea might not have surfaced at all the first time around. By the third session, the amount of new material diminishes rapidly, and a fourth one will usually confirm your suspicion that the subject has been exhausted.

If, however, you want to get contrasting views on the same subject from a number of different segments of the community, you need to multiply the number of interviews by the number of segments. Some of the material will appear repeatedly but you need to keep plugging away if you want to generate ideas and information relating to each of a number of different demographic groups.

Pitfalls

Wells warns of several traps to avoid, and three are particularly important to newspaper editors. First, the glow you get from talking to real live newspaper readers about subjects that are near and dear to your heart is so warm and enchanting that you are very likely to forget that the group interview is one of the world's worst instruments for generating hard information. The interviewees may be so convincing, their information so immediate, that you are deluded into thinking the group is more representative than it really is. No matter how often you remind yourself or the readers of your report that the results are not generalizable, you will find yourself generalizing from them.

It is also important to realize that impressions gleaned from group interviews tend to have a conservative bias. If a new product idea is being tested, interviewees can give a good evaluation of it only if it is something that relates to their own experiences. If it is truly new, the group dynamics will probably inhibit people from playing with the idea, turning it over and examining it, and letting their imaginations range across the possibilities. Ideas that are not easy to explain are severely handicapped in the group situation. If you are trying to predict the effect of radical change, such as electronic delivery of the newspaper, the group interview may lead you to underestimate the possibilities.

A final pitfall to avoid is the tendency of people to want to be nice. Everyone will know that the interview is sponsored by the newspaper and that the interviewer works for the newspaper. If you establish a friendly atmosphere—and you will want to—people may be reluctant to give criticism and negative evaluation. You have to make it clear that you are interested in negative comments and reinforce their awareness of your interest by reacting positively to criticism. If someone says, "The editor should be horsewhipped," just nod your head and say, "Well, yes, that's certainly worth knowing."

All of the above advice applies to those witnesses to the interview who join in during the second half. When they come trooping out from behind the one-way glass, or when the interviewer finally acknowledges their presence and invites them to speak, the best part of the interview is often beginning. It may also be the most dangerous part. I recall one memorable interview in which an editor completely forgot that he was there to receive and not give information and proceeded to use the valuable interview time to set each of the respondents straight on what he regarded as their erroneous thinking about the newspaper. Fortunately, that particular group had been loosened up enough to keep its information flow running, but it could very easily have been chilled for the rest of the evening.

A Final Word of Advice

When important decisions have to be made, never depend on the group interview alone. Use it as a hypothesis-generating device and integrate it into an overall research plan that calls for the really important hypotheses to be treated by rigid methods. If you cannot do this, the risk of being led down the wrong path by the group interview may be so great that it should not be conducted at all.

Appendix: Sample Recruiting Format

Hello. This is _____ from the *Hooverville Herald*. We're talking to people in your area about newspaper reading habits and would like to ask you a few questions. It should only take a couple minutes.

First, how often do you read *The Herald?* Would you say:

almost every day (TERMINATE)

usually (TERMINATE)

only if it looks interesting (CONTINUE)

seldom (CONTINUE)

never (TERMINATE)

(WE'RE TALKING ONLY WITH PEOPLE WHO SELDOM READ OR READ ONLY WHEN IT LOOKS INTERESTING. THANK YOU FOR YOUR TIME.)

Are you employed at least 20 hours per week?

Yes (CONTINUE)

No (TERMINATE)

(WE'RE TALKING ONLY WITH PERSONS EMPLOYED 20 HOURS A WEEK OR
MORE. THANK YOU FOR YOUR TIME.)

Do you or does anyone in your household work for a television station,
a newspaper, public relations firm, a publishing firm, an ad agency, or a
marketing research firm?

Yes (THANK RESPONDENT AND TERMINATE)

No (CONTINUE)

The editors of the *Hooverville Herald* are interested in talking to working women about their newspaper reading habits. We will be conducting
a special kind of marketing research called Focus Group Interviews. This
is a round-table discussion with eight to ten people like yourself. There
are no right or wrong answers. This is strictly a research study and there
are no sales involved. In fact, if you attend the meeting, we will pay you
$25.

The session will last approximately an hour and a half. Could you attend
a meeting on Thursday, Nov. 15th at 7:30?

Yes (CONTINUE)

No (TERMINATE)

The group will meet in the Hooverville Herald building downtown at
One Hoover Plaza. We will be meeting in the Herald dining room on the
third floor.

We would like you to come about 20 minutes early. We will be serving
refreshments.

If you find that you cannot make it or have additional questions, please
call me at 962-4085.

APPLICATIONS / III

The Comic Strip
Problem / 9.

Sooner or later, every editor faces the comic strip problem. While it sounds simple—drop an unpopular strip and pick a popular one—it represents a large and complex class of problems involving the editorial mix. Economists call this process decision making under constraint. Every choice you make narrows your remaining choices. And the trick is to use your finite resources to deliver content that will motivate the largest number of readers to purchase the newspaper. The more you think about this problem, the less simple it becomes.

Thinking of the problem as simple can easily lead an editor astray. When Gary Trudeau took a sabbatical from "Doonesbury" in 1983, editors had to find something to fill the gap. One midwestern editor made his choice by running samples of ten candidates for "Doonesbury's" replacement in the paper and asking readers to tear out a ballot and send it in. The response rate was less than one percent, making it a SSLOP (Self-Selected Loose Opinion Poll) operation, but that was only part of the problem. Not even "Doonesbury" itself is likely to win in even a valid referendum because Trudeau's hip, politically oriented humor appeals to a sophisticated minority. The most popular comics are those with broader appeal: the one-shot gags about kids, pets, and family situations. An editor wishing to maintain the support of the "Doonesbury" market would look for another cartoon with the same satirical spin, such as Berke Breathed's zany "Bloom County."

The editor in this case did include "Bloom County" in his rip-out referendum, but the deck was stacked because the ballot also included some broad-appeal family strips, and "For Better or For Worse," which uses gags based on family situations, won the plurality. If all comics were chosen by referendum, the family gags would be the only comics while reader segments interested in other types went unserved, and that, of course, is what makes the problem complicated. The referendum model doesn't fit.

It may be a better method than rolling dice, but here are some of its hazards:

The least-read comic strip may be followed very intensely by the few who do read it. It might even be their main reason for getting the newspaper.

The least-read strip may be ranked higher by some subgroup that the newspaper's publishing plan has designated as a special target.

The least-read strip might be a key element in some undetected pattern of comic strip preferences. Taking it out may upset an existing balance in this pattern.

Better-read strips may contribute less in net readership because of duplication patterns. The least-read strip is more valuable than it appears if the readers read only it and none other.

The *Philadelphia Inquirer* conducted a comic strip survey designed to deal with each of these possibilities.

Data Collection

A sample of 1,000 home-delivery subscribers was drawn with the help of the circulation department. Each home in the sample was sent 2 questionnaires, 1 to be filled out by any adult and 1 by any child in the household. There were 286 responses, including 51 from children and teenagers. Median age of the sample was 43. Among adults the median age was 50. According to other market surveys, the median age of adult *Inquirer* readers in the Philadelphia SMSA is in the 45–47 range. Because of the low response rate and the bias toward older readers, the sample was not representative of readers in general, but it was a cut above the rip-out polls where respondents are completely self-selected.

The questionnaire allowed respondents to rate each comic strip read on a 7-point scale. A section from each strip was reproduced in the margin to aid in recall. This method produced higher readership figures than an earlier in-home survey in which the respondent was handed a list of strip titles and asked which ones he or she made a point of reading, so it appears that the recall aid is a help.

Factor Analysis

Use of the rating scales makes it possible to search for patterns of readership with factor analysis. This is a standard statistical device for reducing a large number of variables to a few simple clusters. When used to analyze newspaper content, it is a quick way to spot clusters of readership. We define readership as clustered when those people who read one feature in a group tend predictably to read others in the same group. Factor analysis is the device for spotting the groups. In the case of the Philadelphia comics, it turned up three of them:

1. Dramatic serials—People who read "Steve Canyon" tend also to read "Juliet Jones" and the other strips based on a continuing narrative.
2. Sophisticated humor—Readership of 10 strips that seem to share an element of subtlety and occasional social comment was clustered.
3. Light humor—the remaining 13 comics are mainly one-shot sight gags and simple jokes.

If we had started out to classify comic strips without doing a survey at all, we might have discerned the same grouping. But this classification was arrived at by the readers, through their own reading patterns, and is not based directly on the objective characteristics of the strips. It shows that the comic section can be thought of as, in effect, three sections. Taken with what is already known about the need to segment newspaper audiences to appeal to specialized groups, this division suggests that each group of comics ought to be considered separately.

The stability of this kind of grouping can be tested by comparing the Philadelphia factor clusters with those reached by the same method in a different market. A factor analysis of readership of comic strips in *The Miami Herald* revealed the same basic pattern. There were few continued serials in *The Miami Herald* at the time its survey was taken, but those that it did carry landed in the same cluster as the other strips that dealt generally with sports and adventure. There is also a grouping of family comics with simple, one-shot gags and the third group of strips with more sophisticated humor. The Miami findings tend to confirm that there are indeed three separate comic strip audiences.

Managing the Three Groups

Knowing that readers tend to organize their comic-reading habits around these three clusters leads to interesting possibilities. For example, the three types of comics could be segregated on the comic pages so that readers interested primarily in any one type could find all the strips of that kind together. We know from other research that readers tend to scan the newspaper purposively. Anything we can do to improve the newspaper's efficiency as an information-retrieval device will help them and make the newspaper more useful.

Some newspapers have experimented with this kind of clustering and found a graphic drawback. Continued stories have more dialog than the quick gags, and when they are clustered together, the density of the lettering can be offensive to the discriminating eye. Some editors think the extra convenience to the reader makes it worthwhile. The *Washington Post* Sunday comic section is a good example.

Once you start thinking of three segments of comic readers, you have to make a decision on how much space to give to each group. An editor's targeting strategy should play a role here. If there is no special targeting strategy, the number of strips in each category could be adjusted to reflect the proportion of readers primarily interested in each group. This proportional representation scheme has a gut-level appeal and could serve in the absence of a more complicated model.

Each of the Philadelphia respondents was classified as preferring one of the three comic groups by comparing his or her average rating scores for each group. A strip not read counted as zero and was included in the base for averaging. The distribution of preferences is shown in Table 9. In the simplest form of proportional representation, the number of strips in each class would reflect that distribution. Other criteria are possible, however. It might be that the amount of money spent for each strip should be apportioned instead.

It should be remembered, of course, that reader preferences are conditioned to some extent by what they already find in the newspaper. In

TABLE 9

Types of Comics Preferred by
Philadelphia Inquirer Readers

Dramatic serials	28%
Sophisticated humor	23
One-shot gags	47
Unable to classify	2
	100

Miami, for example, readers were offered few continued soap opera strips because editors were aware of their low popularity and gradually weeded them out in deference to the referendum model. The proportion preferring those strips was correspondingly smaller than in Philadelphia, where more of the serials remained. It also might be wise to depart from the proportional representation formula if one of the comic types is favored by a demographic group that the publishing strategy has targeted for developing. The three types of strips do attract somewhat different followings.

Dramatic serials appeal to older readers and long-term readers of the newspaper. It is the only category of comic whose readership is strongly associated with the daily reading habit. The sophisticated humor strips appeal to new readers and young people. They are the favorite of 38% of persons under age 40 compared to only 10% of people who are older. The often-targeted off-and-on readers like this group more than daily readers do. Younger readers are somewhat more drawn to the one-shot gag comics than older readers, especially if they are heavy television viewers. The attraction is fairly even across different levels of education.

Measuring Intensity

With the groupings established, it is easy to rank the different comics within groups by their readership and by the intensity of that readership. This is done in Table 10. Readership is shown as a percent of all persons who can read any comic. The intensity score is simply the average on a 7-point scale among readers of the indicated comic strip. The readership and intensity scores can be combined by multiplying them. This procedure yields an index number that may be thought of as a comic strip's readership discounted by its intensity. A perfect score would be 700, representing a strip that was read by everybody and rated 7 by all of its readers.

The range on the index was from 195 for "Toppix" to 515 for "There Oughta Be a Law." From Table 10 we can see that if we followed the traditional referendum model for dropping comic strips, "Toppix" would be the one to drop. If only intensity were taken into account, "Travels with Farley" would be dropped. Using the index of readership and intensity, "Toppix" would be dropped.

Once the index numbers are established, it is an easy matter to look at

TABLE 10

Readership Rankings within Comic Categories

	Readership	Intensity	Index*
Dick Tracy	70%	4.7	330
Winnie Winkle	68	4.8	325
Gasoline Alley	67	4.5	299
Mark Trail	58	4.8	279
Juliet Jones	53	4.8	251
Steve Canyon	51	4.8	242
Hagar the Horrible	86%	5.5	470
Momma	87	5.2	453
Catfish	77	4.7	366
Animal Crackers	77	4.5	348
Broom Hilda	79	4.2	334
Funky Winkerbean	74	4.1	303
Kelly & Duke	72	3.9	282
Tank McNamara	67	3.9	265
P. T. Bimbo	67	3.7	247
Travels with Farley	56	3.6	200
There Oughta Be A Law	89%	5.8	515
Heathcliff	89	5.6	496
Fred Basset	91	5.4	488
Rivets	88	5.2	455
Charmers	76	5.3	405
Amy	81	4.8	388
Dumplings	78	4.9	382
Freddy	83	4.6	381
Big George	79	4.7	373
A Little Leary	65	5.2	338
Ms. Augusta	73	4.5	328
Toppix	48	4.0	195

*Readership multiplied by Intensity to produce an index of intensity-adjusted readership. Multiplication was performed before rounding the numbers in the first two columns.

them by target group. The case presented here used age and education to define the target groups. An editor interested in reaching a particular group would look for strips that have visibly higher appeal to target group members. For example, "Tank McNamara" has only a mediocre ranking in the referendum reported in Table 10, but scores much higher among young people, particularly college-educated young people. For an editor worried about young readers, "Tank McNamara" would be a much stronger candidate for retention than the referendum indicates.

The McCombs Model

While we have succeeded in complicating what at first glance appeared to be a fairly simple problem, it is possible to complicate matters even more. One factor that should not be overlooked is the degree to which each comic strip attracts a unique audience or an audience that is already drawn to the newspaper by the other comic strips. Maxwell E. McCombs (1977) has proposed a decision model for feature selection that sorts features into four categories: features with high readership that is isolated, i.e., it does not overlap with readership of other features; features with high readership that are clustered with the readership of other features; features of low readership that are isolated; and features with low readership that are clustered.

To use the McCombs model, we must classify the comics according to the extent to which the readership is isolated or clustered. One way to do this is by inspection of the intercorrelations of readership for the strips. But there is an easier way to make this judgment. We have already factor-analyzed the comic ratings, and the factor scores are straightforward indicators of clustering. The higher the factor score for a particular comic, the more than comic's readership correlates with readership of its group as a whole.

For an operational definition, we can classify a comic with a factor score in the top half of its group as clustered and one in the bottom half as isolated. Readership can also be cut at the median for each group. Following this procedure, it is simple to classify each comic according to its position in the McCombs model (Table 11).

The most desirable comics, those with high readership and whose readership is relatively isolated, are "Winnie Winkle," "Dick Tracy," "Gasoline Alley," "Momma," "There Oughta Be a Law," "Rivets," and "Fred Bassett." The least desirable are "Steve Canyon," "Juliet Jones," "Mark Trail," "Funky Winkerbean," "A Little Leary," "Big George," and "Dumplings."

This model can be combined with the referendum model or the proportional representation model to further refine the choices. For example, the proportional representation model tells us that sophisticated humor is over-represented. The only member of this group to fall into the undesirable cell of the McCombs model is "Funky Winkerbean." On the other hand, we might wish to use a simple referendum as the tie breaker in the

TABLE 11

The McCombs Model

	High Readership	Low Readership
	"Winnie Winkle"	"P.T. Bimbo"
	"Dick Tracy"	"Kelly & Duke"
Isolated	"Gasoline Alley"	"Travels with Farley"
	"Momma"	"Tank McNamara"
	"There Oughta Be a Law"	"Ms. Augusta"
	"Rivets"	"Toppix"
	"Fred Bassett"	"Freddy"
	"Broom Hilda"	"Steve Canyon"
	"Catfish"	"Juliet Jones"
	"Animal Crackers"	"Mark Trail"
Clustered	"Hagar the Horrible"	"Funky Winkerbean"
	"Amy"	"A Little Leary"
	"Heathcliff"	"Big George"
	"Charmers"	"Dumplings"

McCombs model, in which case "Steve Canyon" would be dropped because it is the least read of the strips in the undesirable cell of the McCombs model.

These findings apply, of course, only to the Philadelphia market in the middle 1970s. Surveys at other times or in other markets might produce different results.

The Max 4 Model

Modern data processing makes it possible to look at the problem of overlapping readership in a more precise way, provided one has a theory that tells him or her what to look for. Presumably there is a threshold number of comic strips which, if read and given the maximum rating, will cause a reader to stay with the newspaper. A person addicted to less than this threshold number would be significantly more likely to drop the newspaper than a person who is devoted to this number of comic strips or more. It should be possible to design longitudinal research to determine the threshold number.

In the absence of such research, we can only guess, but the guessing game can at least start with an inspection of the number of strips read and given the maximum rating. In the Philadelphia study, the greatest number of people gave the maximum rating to fewer than 3 comic strips.

Another third gave the maximum rating to 3 to 5 comic strips. And the most devoted third bestowed this honor on 6 or more comic strips. The distribution shows a sharp break between 3 and 4 top-rated comic strips, and it therefore seems reasonable to suppose that we ought to make it our goal to have as many people as possible give the maximum rating to at least 4 comic strips.

We can call this model the Max 4 model (Max as in maximum, not Max McCombs). The question then becomes which comic strip can be dropped with the least reduction in the number of readers who give 4 or more comic strips the maximum rating.

This question may be answered through a straightforward simulation of the sort proposed by Jack Haskins (1965) for magazine features. We simply count the number of readers who give the maximum rating to 4 comic strips. Then, for each strip in turn, we discard its top ratings and count the number of top-rated strips remaining for each person. The task is simple enough if one has access to an interactive computer system, thus avoiding the need to make 28 trips to the batch printer. The outcome of these calculations is shown in Table 12. If "Heathcliff" were dropped, the number of people who give the maximum rating to 4 comics would be reduced 8.5%. If "Travels with Farley," "Gasoline Alley," "Amy," or "Top-pix" were dropped, the number of persons showing this intense devotion to at least 4 comics would not be reduced at all.

The Max 4 model can also be combined with other models to break ties. If proportional representation were the tie-breaking criterion, "Travels with Farley" would be dropped because it is a member of an over-represented classification. If the referendum were the tie breaker, "Top-pix" would be dropped.

Bimodal Distributions

One other potential variable, suggested by Mike Kleibrink, ought to be considered. Some newspaper features are controversial, and the controversy draws readers to them irrespective of whether the features are liked. The tipoff is a bimodal distribution in the ratings. If any comic strip has a large number of 1 ratings balanced by a large number of 7 ratings and not very many ratings in the middle, this is a strip that is both loved and hated, and it is read by the holders of both emotions. It would, however, have only a mediocre average. Therefore, it is important to

TABLE 12

The Max 4 Model

"Hagar the Horrible"	6.5%
"Catfish"	4.3
"Momma"	4.3
"Tank McNamara"	3.7
"Animal Crackers"	2.2
"Funky Winkerbean"	2.2
"Broom Hilda"	1.4
"P.T. Bimbo"	0.8
"Kelly & Duke"	0.8
"Travels with Farley"	0
"Juliet Jones"	2.2
"Dicky Tracy"	1.4
Winnie Winkle"	1.4
"Steve Canyon"	0.8
"Mark Trail"	0.8
"Gasoline Alley"	0
"Heathcliff"	8.5
"There Oughta Be a Law"	6.5
"Fred Basset"	5.3
"A Little Leary"	4.3
"Charmers"	3.7
"Dumplings"	3.7
"Rivets"	2.8
"Freddy"	2.2
"Big George"	1.4
"Ms. Augusta"	0.8
"Amy"	0
"Toppix"	0

inspect the frequency distributions. Among the Philadelphia comics, there were 2 basic patterns. A few strips showed normally distributed evaluations. Most were skewed to the low side. In other words, people who read a strip at all tend to like it a lot. There were no cases of a clear bimodal distribution. It seems quite possible, however, that such a distribution might be found for other comics in other newspapers.

Summary

We have in the course of this analysis proposed 8 basic models for rating comic strips. They are summarized in Table 13. In only 1 case does the outcome depart very radically from the outcome of the traditional referendum. "Funky Winkerbean," read by 74% of the comic-reading audience, would not be a likely candidate for dropping if the referendum were the standard. It is the comic to drop if the McCombs model is applied, using the proportional representation rule as the tie breaker.

In all of the other models the comic to drop is one that rates at or near the bottom of the referendum. Editors and researchers who have been choosing comics on the basis of the referendum model may take some comfort in this. It is an easy test to apply, and it is not ambiguous. Not much damage will be done, at least in the short term, if the referendum model is followed. Its chief danger is that it can blind decision makers to the problem of segmentation and the desirability of reaching strategic target groups.

If applied over time, the referendum model would lead to the gradual elimination of the dramatic soap opera strips, and since these strips are associated with retention of the newspaper, that could be a serious mistake. The problem is easily averted, however, by making selections within the three basic groups and taking care always to provide something for the readers of dramatic serials, sophisticated humor, and the simple family strips. Editorial decision makers who lack the resources or the patience for the fine tuning provided by the more complicated models will probably not be led too far astray by the referendum so long as a rough segmentation is maintained.

TABLE 13

Outcomes of the Decision Models

Model	Comic to Drop
1. Referendum	"Toppix"
2. Intensity	"Travels with Farley"
3. Readership/Intensity	"Toppix"
4. McCombs-Referendum	"Steve Canyon"
5. McCombs-P.R.	"Funky Winkerbean"
6. P.R.-Referendum	"Travels with Farley"
7. Max 4-P.R.	"Travels with Farley"
8. Max 4-Referendum	"Toppix"

The Second-Paper Problem / 10.

A second newspaper in a market serves a number of useful social functions. It keeps the staff of the first paper honest and alert. It provides a second chance for interest groups and points of view that get shut out of the first paper. It serves an oversight function with its vested interest in pointing out events and circumstances that the first paper overlooked. And, without question, newspapering is more fun when there is competition. My own most stimulating hours as a reporter came on Saturdays at the *Miami Herald* in the 1950s when the *Miami News* had a competing Sunday paper. Trying to outwrite and outreport a competitor in the same medium on the same cycle of the day makes you energetic and resourceful, and the reader benefits. It is understandably lamented, then, that second papers almost everywhere are in trouble.

Where competing papers are separately owned, the situation can be stable if they are about equal in circulation. But as soon as one begins to dominate, advertisers tend to withdraw their support from the weaker paper, and it begins a downward spiral that ends in an agency agreement, a merger, or closing of the second paper. And where two papers in a market are under the same ownership, the same economic pressures incline the owners to make them uncompetitive by combining their newsside functions to some degree. This chapter is about the different ways of structuring two newspapers in a one-owner market and some of the costs and benefits of the different configurations.

The owner of two newspapers in a single market has a large variety of possible operating modes. The key variable that distinguishes these modes is the amount of integration of the newsroom operations. Decisions about how to organize the business-side functions, production, circulation, and advertising, must all flow from the original decision on newsroom operation. Theoretically, the number of possible varieties is close to infinite. At one extreme, you can have totally separate and bitterly competitive newsrooms, like those of the *Charlotte News* and the *Charlotte Observer* before 1984. At the other extreme is the case of two newspapers merged into a single operation publishing on only one cycle, usually morning. The *Minneapolis Star and Tribune* after 1982 is an example. In between, the number of possibilities is limited only by management's imagination. However, these middle categories can be divided roughly into two groups according to the amount of newsroom integration. For this analysis, integration is "low" if less than half of the type from the paper on one cycle is picked up by the paper on the other cycle.

If a majority of content from one paper is picked up by the other, integration is high. Generally, it is the afternoon paper that picks up the morning paper's copy. If the two papers have the same name and graphic design so that a reader cannot tell by looking at one whether it is the morning or evening edition, it is classed, by the definition of the Audit Bureau of Circulation, as an all-day paper. However, some papers are organized exactly like all-day papers but change the name and/or the graphic design between cycles and are therefore all-day papers disguised as something else.

In sum, then, there are four basic ways to organize a two-paper, one-owner situation:

1. Keep them at arm's length from each other and bitterly competitive. Example: The *Kansas City Star* and *Times* under editor Michael Davies in the 1980s.

2. Combine some newsroom functions and have the papers share some type. Example: The *San Jose Mercury* and *News* under executive editor Larry Jinks in the 1970s.

3. Combine most or all newsroom functions and share most of the type. Example: The morning and evening editions of the *Boston Globe* under executive editor Robert H. Phelps in the late 1970s and early 1980s.

4. Merge the two into one paper on one cycle. Generally, this means killing the weaker paper, although its name may survive for a time in a hyphenated masthead. Example: The *Des Moines Register and Tribune* under editor Michael Gartner in the 1980s.

If there were one best way to organize two papers in a single market, owners would have surely discovered it by now. The fact that such a variety exists suggests that local factors, including the papers' own history, have a lot to do with the form that emerges. Any attempt to develop a formula for fitting an operating mode to the needs of a given market should begin with an examination of the most common modes, their benefits, and their costs.

An ideal form of organization would achieve the following goals:

1. Improve circulation.
2. Maximize average daily net readership, i.e., the number of people who read at least one newspaper, or "net reach."
3. Protect the market from the entry of new competition.
4. Optimize production, circulation, and advertising efficiency.

Traditional wisdom in the newspaper business holds that the first three goals are best met by keeping the two papers in a scrappy, competitive relationship, and that these benefits come at the expense of the fourth. If efficiency were the only goal, one paper would be better than two, and a highly integrated combination would be better than one with little or no integration. But the other goals may seem so important that some inefficiency is justified. Two separate newsrooms fighting for the attention of the reader are more likely to get it, the theory goes, than a noncompetitive newsroom. Two different papers will yield more total circulation than one paper or two similar papers, because some people will want to read both. And the number who read at least one is maximized because two different papers can attract two different kinds of audiences, appealing to each more fully than a single paper could. If both evening and morning fields are covered, there is less incentive for a competitor to try something new in the market.

An Empirical Test

All of this sounds plausible, even obvious. But is it true? Efforts to test some of these propositions with empirical research have been made. Circulation data is available for all daily newspapers, so it is fairly easy to compare the circulation performance of papers with different modes or organization. Comparing the effect on net reach is more difficult. Reach is measured by sample surveys, and many newspapers either do not conduct such surveys frequently, or they do so but keep the results under wraps. To measure the effect of different organizational structures on protection of the market and operating efficiency is even more difficult.

For studying these outcomes, there is little to go on but case-study material and common sense.

For a crude affirmation of the theory that competitive newspapers encourage circulation, we need only look at those cases where newspapers have died. In every case, the lost circulation of a failed newspaper has never been fully captured by its survivors. In Chicago, for example, the competitive one-owner combination of the *Tribune* and *Today* had a total circulation of 1.3 million before *Today* was killed. After a year of trying to woo the former *Today* buyers, the *Tribune* had a circulation of only 751,000. In terms of total major daily circulation (the *Sun-Times* and *Daily News* were still in the field), the Chicago loss was 20%.

What about net readership? That went down, too, although not by as much, since some of the lost *Today* circulation had been going to duplicate readers. In the spring of 1973, the Chicago market had 65.4% of adults reading at least 1 of the major dailies on an average day. Two years later, with *Today* gone, that net readership was down to 58.8%, a relative drop of 10%. It left some 300,000 persons in the Chicago area who were not then, but had been, newspaper readers.

The evidence is therefore quite strong that two papers are better than one when maximum circulation is the goal. Moreover, two are probably better than one when net readership is the goal. But the extreme case of the death of a newspaper does not tell us anything about the more subtle options: two papers in a competitive relationship compared to two papers with some degree of integration in their news operations. Fortunately, research is available on that subject.

Three journalism professors, David H. Weaver, John C. Schweitzer, and Gerald C. Stone (1977), looked at 96 two-paper, one-owner markets and classified each market according to how similar the two papers were. If the perceived virtues of separate news operations were real, the combinations with the greatest differences between the two papers should have had the greatest ratio of circulation to households—called penetration by the marketing people.

They found instead a small tendency in the other direction. Newspaper combinations with the best circulation performance tended to be those where the two papers were similar. Their study was criticized, however, for failing to take into account the wide variation in size among their 96 markets. Larger markets tend to have lower penetration because they are more diverse communities with more competition from other kinds of

TABLE 14

Penetration by Type of Newsroom by Size of Market

Top 100 Markets

	Median Penetration
Same editor (12 cases)	.28
Different editor (40 cases)	.63
Second 100 Markets	
Same editor (14 cases)	.70
Different editor (29 cases)	.73
Third 100 Markets	
Same editor (10 cases)	.82
Different editor (10 cases)	.83

media, particularly suburban papers, and more delivery problems over their wider areas. Larger markets are also more likely, for a variety of historic reasons, to have their two-paper combinations managed to produce different kinds of products. We would therefore expect, with all other things being equal, to find that two-paper combinations with low news-editorial integration have lower penetration simply because they tend to be found in the larger markets. The three professors did find this, but because the tendency was so slight in view of the market differences, the suspicion arises that something else is going on.

A Deeper Look

The search was continued by Clyde Z. Nunn (1978) of the Newspaper Advertising Bureau, who studied 115 two-paper situations and classified them according to whether the newsrooms were integrated or separate. He used a simple operational definition of integration: newsrooms were integrated if the morning and evening papers listed the same managing editor in the *Editor and Publisher Yearbook*. They were classed as separate if they had different editors. While there may be a few newsroom organizational schemes sufficiently complicated to defy such easy classification, his operationalization makes sense. Nunn avoided the problem of letting market size confound the findings by holding that factor constant. He did this by looking at the largest 100 markets separately, then the second 100 and the third 100. He found a difference opposite to that noted by the three professors. Among newspapers in markets of roughly equal size, Nunn found that the papers with separate managing editors had the penetration edge. The difference was small in all but the largest markets, as Table 14 shows.

So it appears that conventional thinking about two-paper situations is correct. Separate the editorial staffs, and you get higher penetration, at least in the largest markets. However, causation could run in the other direction. It may be that the newspapers in the high-penetration markets, by virtue of their success, have been slower to change from traditional modes of operation. Perhaps low penetration is the cause of newsroom integration rather than the other way around. The direction of causation cannot be detected by a one-time cross-sectional study. A longitudinal study, i.e., one with measures at different times, is needed.

Fortunately, Nunn's data did show circulation for two years, 1970 and 1976, and he was kind enough to permit a secondary analysis. In my analysis, circulation change, not penetration at one time, was the target. It used 87 cases where the same form of news organization was in place at both the beginning and the end of the period. Because the form of organization existed before the circulation trend, it could not be an effect of circulation. Once again, size was held constant. Table 15 is the result of that analysis.

In the larger markets, the conventional wisdom remains undisturbed. Papers with editorial separation did better than those news operations were combined under a single editor. However, for the smaller markets, there is a dramatic difference. Those who had combined their news operations outperformed the others and gained circulation in a period when

TABLE 15

Circulation Change 1970–1976
by Type of Newsroom and Market Size

Top 100 Markets
	Median Circulation Change
Same editor (8 cases)	−4.9%
Different editors (32 cases)	−3.5

Second 100 Markets
| Same editor (8 cases) | −5.7% |
| Different editors (21 cases) | 3.5 |

Third 100 Markets
| Same editor (10 cases) | 7.0% |
| Different editors (8 cases) | −0.2 |

the industry as a whole was losing it. In the industry as a whole, the loss was 1.8%. In the 115 2-paper markets, the median loss was 3.3%. (Two-paper markets are more vulnerable to circulation loss because duplicate readers tend to give up 1 paper in times of economic difficulty.)

This outcome is not as counterintuitive as it might seem. Bigger cities with diverse populations can support diversity in their media. In smaller markets with homogeneous populations, the efficiencies of combined news operations may have the better payoff. The conventonal wisdom works for the larger newspaper operations, but not for the smaller. Perhaps the conventional wisdom is unduly influenced by the larger and more visible cases. More importantly, it may be that what happened in the smaller markets in the 1970s began to happen later in the larger markets as intramedia competition increased and advertisers withdrew their support for second papers.

Evaluating Duplication

Regardless of the size of the market, whether a second paper survives or not depends in large degree on the attitude of its advertisers. The most sophisticated advertisers, those with the responsibility for placing the advertising for national corporations, prefer fewer newspapers, more penetration, and less duplication. This is their preference even in cases where a second paper makes a clear contribution to net readership. Their reasoning is that a second paper encourages duplicate readership, and that duplication eats up newsprint and ink whose cost is necessarily passed through to the advertisers. These are people who know how to count and measure, skills that are crucial for spreading an advertising budget across a wide variety of media, and they believe that they are spending the print portions of their budgets most efficiently when they reach every household once. For a second paper to make any sense at all to them, it has to reach a largely unduplicated audience. Therefore, any newspaper manager evaluating a two-paper operation should look first at the extent of duplication.

In general, duplication will be less if the two papers are unequal in size. One way to evaluate duplication in a given market is to compare it to a probability model given the existing total readership of each paper. Consider this illustration:

		Morning Readers	
		Yes	No
Evening Readers	Yes	A	B
	No	C	D

The total $A + C$ is the morning readership and $A + B$ the evening readership, while cell A represents duplicate readership. Fill the table with percentages for your market based on the total adult audience so that $A + B + C + D = 100$.

To see how far duplication in your market deviates from what would occur by chance given the relative size of the readership of each paper, make the following calculation:

$$P = (A + C) * (A + B) / 100$$

This gives you the expected value for cell A, the duplicate readers as a percent of the total market. Most two-newspaper markets have a level of duplication that is very close to the probability model. If yours is not, you should ask yourself what historic or policy factors have made it that way, and whether the difference is in the direction you would like it to be.

The next thing to calculate is the contribution to net readership made by the weaker paper. Use this calculation when the weaker paper is the one published in the evening:

$$N = B/(A + C)$$

N is the net addition, in terms of percentage increase, to the morning paper's reach produced by the evening paper. If the evening paper is the stronger, the equation of course becomes:

$$N = C/(A + B)$$

Here is how this calculation can be used to make some real-life comparisons:

Second Paper's Contribution to Average Daily Readership

	Stronger Paper	Combination	Difference	% Difference
Market A	40%	61%	21%	52%
Market B	27	37	10	37
Market C	43	56	13	30
Market D	65	71	6	9

These numbers are based on average daily readership calculated from the "read yesterday" question in market surveys. They show there is extreme variation among markets in duplicated readership. In Market A, the second paper extends the combination's reach by more than half, so its economic justification seems assured. In Market D, net reach would be impressive with or without the second paper.

The Reach-Cost Ratio

Once you have calculated the net additional reach provided by a second paper, you are in a good position to evaluate it by comparing its contribution to net reach to its cost. Unfortunately, finding out its cost is not as easy as it sounds. The cost you are interested in is the incremental cost, i.e., the amount of additional money spent to produce and distribute the second paper once you are already committed to producing and distributing the first paper. This amount is always less than the proportional cost of the second paper based on circulation because most of the fixed costs are charged to the first paper. Once you have paid for the building, the printing press and the typesetting equipment for the first paper, you can use them again for the second paper at very little additional cost. The press may wear out sooner if you print two papers on it instead of one, but the cost of that additional wear is trivial. Technological obsolescence is far more detrimental to the value of the press than is continuous use.

The main costs of a second paper are the variable costs, those that depend on how many units are produced. For a newspaper company, the main variable costs are newsprint, ink, and transportation. These costs increase in fairly direct proportion to circulation.

Newspaper accounting systems are not normally organized to yield the incremental cost of a second paper, but it can be calculated with a special study that examines each cost of the total operation and asks what would happen to that cost if there were no second paper. I have encountered a few cases where such special studies were done, and from them derived a rule of thumb that gives a rough approximation. The rule is that a company that owns the facilities for producing 1 paper can put out a second one of equal circulation on the opposite cycle for an additional cost equal to about 30% of the cost of the first paper. If the second paper is smaller in circulation, the cost is reduced in proportion to the second paper's share of the total circulation of the combination. If you are more comfortable with an equation, it looks like this:

$$\frac{30}{.5} = \frac{X}{S}$$

where S is the second paper's share of total circulation and X is the incremental cost of that circulation. That equation can be simplified to

$$X = 60 * S$$

and it allows for some economies of scale as the second paper gets bigger. Individual situations will differ, of course, and there is no substitute for an internal accounting of every cost. This is an important exercise in evaluating a second paper because you can use it to compare the marginal reach contributed by a second paper to its marginal cost. A second paper that adds 52% to the net reach in a given market at an additional cost of only 21% would have a reach-cost ratio of 2.5 to 1, and its owners can take comfort in that. On the other hand, a paper that adds only 9% to net reach but 16% to total cost has a negative reach-cost ratio and is ripe for a change.

Reasons to Merge

Unless the second paper is extremely low in circulation, the main cost savings through integration of operations is in newsprint. The newsroom is not a good place to look for cost-cutting opportunities for several reasons. In the first place, the newsroom is a relatively minor cost center, particularly on larger papers. In general, newsroom costs will eat up only from 5 to 15% of operating revenues, depending on circulation size. The relative cost is less for large papers because the need for reporters and editors is only loosely linked to circulation size. If your paper doubled its circulation tomorrow, you could still produce it with the same news staff.

Another reason that the newsroom is a poor place to look for cost savings is that the newsroom of the second paper in a fully separated 2-paper operation is generally smaller and operates on a lower budget than that of the larger paper, generally from 20 to 30% of the combination's total news-editorial expenses. This saving can be made only when the integration move is extreme, from a totally competitive mode to a total merger that wipes out the second newsroom. Most owners prefer less drastic moves, from total competition to some degree of integration, and the potential saving is accordingly smaller.

A better reason to merge two papers is to save newsprint by eliminating the duplicate readership. Even that goal can involve some ambiguous tradeoffs. They stem from the attitudes of advertisers.

In recent years, newspaper readership has been in a gradual decline while circulation has generally been rising. The rise, of course, has been due to population growth, and ad salesmen like to point to the growing circulation, hoping that the advertiser won't notice that it is not increasing as fast as the number of households. Such a hope is increasingly futile as local shop owners are supplanted by managers for national retail chains and franchisees who bring the national organization's sophistication to their ad-buying decisions. Nevertheless, it can be difficult for a newspaper that has always stressed its growing circulation to suddenly take a step to reduce that circulation by wiping out the duplicate readership.

Advertisers are glad to see the duplication go because they believe that getting the message into one home twice is a waste of their money. They may be right, although the evidence is not certain on this point. Not every ad is read by every person who gets a newspaper, and repeated exposure should increase the effective reach. And there is some evidence that repeated messages have more impact than one-shot efforts. Buyers of advertising space are often forced to overlook these subtleties, however, because of the complexities of allocating their ad dollars across the great variety of media available today. To make these choices, they use some very simple models that measure something called "combined reach," which is the total number of different individuals reached once with an advertising message. From their point of view, figuring out how to reach the maximum number of people through print, radio, and TV is complicated enough without having to worry about the benefit of a second major newspaper in town.

This attitude on the part of advertisers explains why it is so much easier to kill a weak second paper than it used to be. If there is high duplication, circulation will go down, but the advertiser, knowing that he still has the same net reach, will willingly pay close to the same rate.

For the circulation department, a two-paper situation can be excruciatingly frustrating. The impulse is generally to promote the second paper in a never-ending effort to bring it to parity with the strong paper. There is no very good reason for such a strategy except perhaps for the psychological satisfaction of achieving a symmetrical relationship. Indeed, such a strategy works against the rational aim of reducing duplication. When two papers are close to the same size, as we have already seen in the probability model, the opportunities for duplication are maximized. When one paper is much stronger than the other, there are mathematically fewer opportunities for duplication. The antiduplication tactic would be to allow a fading second paper to decline while replacing its losses by building up the stronger paper. Eventually, the second paper would either find its hard core of special-interest readers or sink so low that it could disappear without leaving much of a ripple. A two-paper ownership that spends all of its energies trying to maintain an unnatural balance will find itself unable to cope with more urgent problems.

The Options

Given all that is happening in the world today, what are the realistic options for the owner of two papers in one market? Most of the possibilities will fit one of the following models:

1. *The specialized second paper.* This is the age of specialization in media. Therefore, if you are going to have two papers, you might as well design them for different kinds of people. The trouble with this theory is that there are many more than two different kinds of people, and a second paper does not really provide that much opportunity for specialization.

For such a strategy to work, the second paper needs to find an audience that advertisers want to reach and that cannot be reached as efficiently through a more general medium. It has been tried. There are no very impressive success stories. The *Miami News* tried to halt its circulation slide by positioning itself as the newspaper for TV watchers. It didn't help. The *Minneapolis Star* tried a magazine format for unhurried readers. It merely alienated old readers without attracting new ones.

Perhaps no one has yet found the right speciality for the second paper.

An extremely narrow speciality might work. The *Pasadena Star-News* experimented with a special all-sports edition. Perhaps second papers could be converted into racing forms, business papers, or lonely-hearts exchanges. But then they would be entering a different kind of business altogether.

2. *The integrated newsroom.* Keeping two papers for tradition's sake but saving newsroom costs by combining the newsrooms is a popular but generally temporary move. It is popular with owners because the public cannot readily perceive the effects of the change. And by sharing a certain amount of type, two formerly separate papers can begin to discourage the duplicate readers, who will begin to notice that they are paying for the same stories twice. But the newsroom cost savings are not great, and this is a painfully slow way to reduce duplication. If the papers have historically been different, the task of managing the two with one staff is difficult and painful. An editor who tries it has to be "a functional schizophrenic," according to James Hoge, who once faced that task when he simultaneously edited the *Chicago Sun-Times* and the dying *Chicago Daily News.* And the experience is hard on staff members, who have to become more like wire service reporters and work against deadlines around the clock, producing a.m. and p.m. angles for every story.

3. *The all-day format.* The frustrations of two papers and one staff can be eased by dropping the effort to produce two distinctive papers and concentrating on one paper that is delivered in two cycles. This takes care of most of the duplication problem. The reader no longer has a choice of papers, but does have the choice of delivery in the morning or evening. A diehard few will still insist on getting both papers.

4. *Merger.* What this really means, of course, is killing the weaker paper. This solution has the advantage of being straightforward. There is no temptation to hide what you are doing. Duplication is automatically eliminated forever. It is painful for the news-editorial people, but, if the operation is well managed, it can lead to a reallocation of resources that will make the one surviving paper so much better than either paper was before that everyone will wonder why the move wasn't made years earlier.

A Stronger Editorial Product

Enlightened newspaper owners recognize the importance of a strong editorial product in maintaining their competitive edge against the proliferation of other kinds of media that modern technology has made possible. Those who can't or don't wish to see as far ahead worry more about the next quarter's bottom line. The way a consolidation of two papers is handled tells a reader all he has to know about the kind of ownership which is serving him. A short-sighted owner will lay off staff and pass the gains straight through to the bottom line. Owners with more vision realize that the way to cope with the market for specialized information is to make a strong central-city newspaper a cafeteria of specialized information. The staff strength that can be gained through consolidation can be applied to making the staff more specialized, producing more and better information of a more specialized nature.

When the *Roanoke Times & World-News* changed from separate operations to a modified all-day format in 1977, all of the savings were put into an expanded and improved editorial product. The two education reporters, instead of covering the same meetings in competition, divided into subspecialties, with one tackling the public schools and the other going after higher education. Readers got features from both papers, including two advice columnists. The local columnists found their audiences greatly expanded.

What it comes down to is a question of managing resources. With so many nonnewspaper media coming at the traditional newspaper advertising base, building and keeping reader loyalty is more important than ever before. A big, high-quality editorial product edited for a diversity of interests is essential. The resources to upgrade existing products have to come from somewhere, and consolidation of two-paper operations is one sure-fire way to get them. One good paper is a better defense against these new threats than two mediocre papers or one pretty good paper and one that is fading away. It used to be thought that a two-paper combination had to hold on to its second paper in order to prevent competition from entering the field on the second-paper cycle. That is no longer much of a worry. It is now beginning to appear that the best way to cope with potential or existing competition is to put all of your resources into one editorial product and to make that product the best you can possibly produce.

Let us therefore not lament the passing of the second papers or the decline of intra-ownership competition. To compete with the real foes on the outside, newspaper companies need to become more integrated and cooperative on the inside.

Advertising / 11.
Research

Historically, most newspaper marketing research has been advertising research. Even when newspaper owners could take the readers for granted, they still had to sell the advertisers, and sound research proved to be a useful selling tool. When interest in marketing to readers as well as to advertisers developed in the late 1960s, researchers had an existing body of methodology and standardized procedure to build on. It is worth knowing a little bit about the advertising research tradition even if your main interest is news-editorial research.

One reason is that a lot of the things that newspaper research departments do out of habit and tradition were designed expressly to meet some limited advertising applications and may not necessarily be the best things to do when readership is the object of study. By tracing these procedures to their origins, the news researcher can better understand and evaluate them.

Another reason is the economic advantage of the multipurpose study. When funds are not available for a study devoted solely to readership, a study that serves both advertising and readership goals can sometimes be designed. Anyone working on the readership portion of such a study can do a better job if he or she understands what the folks on the advertising side are trying to do.

The basic goal of advertising research is to tell the advertiser about the audience he is buying. And the first thing the advertiser wants to know is the size of that audience. Circulation used to be the main indicator of audience size. Divided by households to yield household penetration, it told the advertiser how much of the market was being reached and how one newspaper compared to another. With circulation failing to keep up with the growth in the number of households, however, newspapers have been harder pressed to justify their worth and have turned to indicators that contain more information than does the raw circulation figure.

The basic measure of advertising research that has resulted is called average daily readership or, after the question used to measure it, "read yesterday." It was developed after considerable experimentation to provide a credible, conservative estimate of readership, and, if you have not encountered it before, you will be surprised at its complexity. Many people on the news side see the world as divided into two kinds of people, readers and nonreaders. If that were true, all you would need to do to find out which a given person was would be to ask him or her. The truth, of course, is that almost everyone is a reader some of the time, and people vary greatly in their frequency of newspaper readership. Defining the cutting point between a reader and a nonreader can be quite complicated.

To the advertiser, however, this is more a philosophical than a practical question. What he or she wants to know is how many people will be exposed to the ad on a given day. The aim, then, is not so much to try to classify levels of readership as to simply know how many readers there are on an average day. "Yesterday" is asked about in order to yield that average. "Yesterday" is a specific 24-hour period, easily understood, and within the accurate recall of most respondents. When the question is asked of an equal number on successive days, Tuesday through Saturday, the result is an average for the five weekdays.

Interview respondents are sometimes tempted to exaggerate their socially approved behavior, and newspaper reading is a sign of some sophistication. It demonstrates that one can, indeed, read, and it suggests the ability to understand and reflect on the complicated events of the day. Most people would rather be known as readers than nonreaders, and so a way had to be found to ask the question without tempting the respondent to inflate the response. The "read yesterday" question does this by backing into the issue so unobtrusively that the respondent doesn't realize when he is being classified.

The question typically begins with an introductory discussion of newspaper reading habits and the varieties of reading behavior. This part of the question is not standardized. Its function is to suggest that all varieties of reading behavior are socially acceptable. The respondent is next given a number of opportunities to confess, in a nonhumiliating way, that he is among the nonreaders. A typical series might go like this:

"Let's talk about several papers that you may or may not have read. Have you ever read the *Miami Journal?*"

If the respondent says no, that is that, and the interviewer changes the subject. If he or she has read the *Miami Journal,* this question is asked:

"Within the past week, have you read or looked into a weekday copy—that is, a Monday to Friday copy—of the *Miami Journal?*"

If no, the respondent is shunted out of this series. If yes, it is on to the next hurdle:

"When was the last time you read or looked into any weekday copy of the *Miami Journal?*"

Often, the respondent will recall reading one "today." If so, he or she is asked, "And when was the last time before today?"

Whether he read today or not, the trap is now sprung. If the respondent read "yesterday" (or "Friday" if the interview is conducted on a Monday), he or she is classed as a yesterday reader. If the last time before today was some day other than the previous weekday, the person goes into the record as not being a yesterday reader. Add them all up, make sure that the same number of interviews was collected on each day of the week (or weight the data to bring the days into equal balance), and you have average daily readership. The person who did not read yesterday is not humiliated, and you have a good, precise measure.

For Sunday readership, the procedure is the same except that readership is first asked about for any of the past four Sundays and then for last Sunday.

This measure can be used to compare one newspaper with another and the same newspaper with itself at different times. For the advertiser, it can be cross-tabulated by demographic data or information about purchasing habits. If the advertiser wants to know how many patrons of a particular shopping center or how many 20- to 40-year-old tennis players read the paper on an average day, this procedure, if the sample is large enough, can tell him.

Newspaper researchers are justly proud of the "read yesterday" measure, for it is a model of good methodology. However, it is also a good example of a procedure developed for the advertising side that is not as useful when applied to readership research. Here's why:

In readership research, we are primarily interested in distinguishing between frequent readers and those who are not so frequent. As has already been demonstrated, converting the hard-core nonreader to readership is not nearly as easy or desirable as increasing the frequency of the sometime reader. To do that, you need a measure, a dependent variable, that sorts people into categories according to their readership frequency. "Read yestereday" does not do that. It pulls all of the yesterday readers into its net, including those who read every day and those who read only once a week but for whom "yesterday" happened to be the day.

If you had a very large sample, that might not be much of a problem, because yesterday readership certainly correlates with frequent readership. It has to by virtue of the fact that the frequent reader has a much higher probability of being caught in yesterday's net. But most market studies have small samples, and to make them efficient, you need as clean a measure as you can devise.

Framing the question in terms of very specific behavior is still a good idea, so a question that asks about the past five weekdays—or in the case of a Sunday paper, about the last four Sundays—will do the job. "Out of the last five weekdays, that is Monday through Friday, on how many days did you read or look into the *Miami Journal?*" In a multipurpose survey, this should be asked after the read-yesterday series so as not to bias the response for the critical advertising measure. The researcher can then look at the distribution and set the cutting points where it is most convenient for the analytical problem at hand.

Or, where comparability with national data is desired, the readership question of the National Opinion Research Center of the University of Chicago can be adapted to local use: "How often do you read the newspaper — every day, a few times a week, once a week, less than once a week, or never?" The problem with this question is that it does not force the respondent to think about specific behavior at a specified time and is therefore more subject to errors of memory and interpretation.

There may be occasions when a news problem is tackled with secondary research on a survey done primarily for advertisers, and "read yesterday" is the only readership question that was asked. Use it. But when you have a chance to participate in the design of a multipurpose study, get another readership question into the package, too.

Average daily readership measures "reach," which is advertising jargon for the number of unduplicated individuals who are exposed to the message at least once. It is the basis for a useful sales tool for the advertising department: the ability to demonstrate how the number of unduplicated readers is affected by the frequency with which the ad appears.

Suppose that on an average weekday, 50% of the adults in your market see your newspaper. For 1 ad appearing on 1 day, the reach is 50%. (We are not claiming that 50% see the ad in question—just as television broadcasters do not claim that everyone who has the set turned on stays in the room for the commercial. Some advertising researchers do worry about such questions, but they introduce another level of expense and complexity.) Now suppose that the advertiser is persuaded to place the message in the paper on 2 of the 5 weekdays instead of 1. What will his reach be then? Chances are that it will be higher. Because any given day's readership includes some people who see the paper less than daily, a second exposure will always pick up some readers who were missed the first time. This added pickup of readers is called the "cume" (for cumulative readership), and a good deal of effort in newspaper advertising readership is devoted to demonstrating how a newspaper audience accumulates across more than 1 day's edition.

This idea of the cume becomes more important as reading frequency declines. If everybody reads the paper every day, there is no cume. Everybody gets the message the first time it goes out. But if the audience consists mostly of people who read two or three times a week, the cume will be steep. The irony for the advertiser is that the more newspaper readership declines, the more ads he has to buy to accumulate the same audience.

How is the cume measured? There is no very good way. Ideally, we would do repeated surveys of the same individuals, asking them every day for a week if they had read "yesterday." Then we could observe directly how many individuals were added to the cume with each successive insertion of the ad. Such repeated interviewing is, of course, wildly impractical. Not only would it be expensive, but it would make the respondents so self-conscious about their reading behavior that they would change that behavior—probably in the direction of reading more. What is often done instead is to interview each individual twice. Then, on the basis of the "read yesterday" answers for those two days, projections to five days are made to fit some prior assumptions built into a mathematical model. There are several such models, and some of them work on hand calculators.

Another and cheaper way to do the job is to ask the respondent specifically about each of the previous five week days and build the cumes from that information. The trouble with this method from the advertising department's point of view is that respondents don't always remember whether they have read the paper on each of the last five week days. Can you? And they tend to be conservative and under-report their reading.

The solution to this difficulty is to estimate the loss from this source and crank in an arbitrary correction factor to make up for it. Unfortunately, some research suppliers with this method find that it occasionally yields cumes greater than 100 percent of the audience, a result that causes some embarrassment and impedes credibility.

The going really gets murky when advertising researchers try to estimate the cume across different kinds of media. Suppose, for example, that you buy an ad in a newspaper that reaches 50% of the adults in a market and then add a TV spot in prime time on a show that reaches 30%. What has been your net reach? If all newspaper readers avoided television and all TV watchers never looked at newspapers, the answer would be easy: 80%. But, of course, there is some overlap. One way to estimate it is to use a probability model. Assume that for each individual in the audience, the probabilities of reading that newspaper and watching that TV show are independent.

You don't need an equation to see how it works. Think of it this way. A random adult has a 50% chance of *not* reading the newspaper that day and a 70% chance of *not* seeing the TV show. The probability that he or she won't do either is a 50% chance of a 70% chance, or a probability of 35%. If the probability of not getting the message is 35%, the probability of getting it has to be 65%. This means that you could expect 65% of the adults in the market to either read the newspaper or watch the TV show or do both. An advertiser who has that figured out can then compare the payoff between 2 newspaper ads, 2 TV ads, or 2 of each. For those who prefer to think in an equation, here it is:

$$\text{Cume} = 1 - (1 - A) * (1 - B)$$

where A is the newspaper reach and B is the TV reach. Therefore,

$$\text{Cume} = 1 - (1 - .5) * (1 - .3) \text{ or } 1 - (.5 * .7) = .65$$

The trouble with this model is that TV viewing and newspaper reading are not independent. Users of one medium tend to be (or sometimes not to be, depending on the content) users of another. But the probability model provides a starting point for making estimates.

Survey data can be used to generate more accurate intermedia comparisons. The apples-and-oranges problem is horrendous. Whether or not a respondent looked at a newspaper on a given day is unambiguous. But what is the broadcast equivalent of "read yesterday"? It is not watched TV yesterday, nor even watched a particular channel yesterday. You may convince an advertiser that everyone who picks up the paper is going to see his ad, but you can't credibly claim that everyone who tunes in a particular channel on a given day is going to see every advertising message broadcast that day.

To cope with this problem, advertising researchers have broken the television broadcast day into segments called "dayparts." These dayparts are separated by cutting points set to define fairly homogeneous audiences. Seven dayparts are commonly used, although they do not account for the entire day. Daytime television, from 10 in the morning to 4:30 in the afternoon, which includes the female soap-opera viewers, is one. Weekend afternoons, from 2 to 5, when men watch sports, is another. Then, of course, there is prime-time, which is defined as 8 to 11 p.m. Monday through Saturday and 7 to 11 p.m. on Sunday.

Then there is early fringe, defined as 4:30 to 7:30 on weekdays; prime access, the half-hour before prime-time; late fringe, from 11 p.m. to 1 a.m. every night of the week, and weekend children's time, 8 a.m. to 2 p.m. on weekends (Surmanek, 1980).

Radio has dayparts, too. From 6 to 10 a.m. is the a.m. drive time. Then comes housewife time until 3 when p.m. drive time starts. From 7 to midnight is nighttime.

These dayparts, defined here by Eastern Standard Time, are used for very general evaluations of audience levels, viewing patterns, demographics and cost estimates. Once a media buyer gets down to negotiating for a specific time period he or she will look at finer segments, down to the half-hour and the demographics that will tell how many people of a given target audience to expect within each period.

Dayparts can be asked about in the same sample surveys that ask the read-yesterday question to get estimates of the cumulative effect of different media. They can also be used to make some impressive comparisons of the cost-effectiveness of different kinds of media. An advertiser who is bent on using television can sometimes be shown that dividing his budget between the newspaper and TV will reach a larger (and more desirable) audience than he would obtain if he spent the whole wad on television. Of course, the apples-and-oranges problem never goes away entirely. Do you compare, for example, a 30-second spot on the local news with a quarter-page ad in the A section or with a half page? Your choice may make all the difference when bottom-line cost-effectiveness is defined.

In an effort to make better apples-to-oranges comparisons, media planners have adopted some basic concepts that are frequently used in newspaper research. News-side researchers who work on omnibus surveys should learn them in order to converse easily with the folks on the advertising side.

A basic unit of measurement, originating in broadcast research, is the rating. It is defined as the percentage of homes with television (or radio) sets receiving a given program. If half of all TV homes watch the president's news conference, its rating is 50. Advertisers like high ratings, so networks strive to provide programs that will be watched by large numbers of people. Mass appeal is worth more than specialized appeal.

When the networks compete with each other for the biggest ratings, they are interested in market share, a concept from package goods marketing. Its logic says that instead of worrying about the size of the pie, you should devote some attention to size of your slice relative to everybody else's slice. To define market share, the base is changed from all homes with television to all homes that have television *and* are using it at the time being measured. This base is called HUT, for Homes Using Television, and it measures the size of the pie at any given moment. Using HUT as the base makes it possible to compare the relative success of programs broadcast at different times of the day as the size of the audience grows and declines. HUT peaks in the winter months and the evening hours. It is beginning to decline as owners of TV sets find other uses for the tube, including games, recordings, computer display, and videotex reception.

What does all of this have to do with newspapers? Quite a bit. Newspapers can have ratings, too. Average daily readership is a rating of sorts because it is expressed as a percentage of all adults in the market. Therefore, an ad in a paper with an average daily readership of 50% can be viewed as the rough equivalent of a TV commercial on a program with a rating of 50%. It is only a rough equivalent because the base changes: households in the case of the TV rating and individuals in the case of the newspaper measurement. One can be converted to the other because the surveys that measure households also measure the number of people in those households. As measures of advertising messages received, they are still rough estimates, because neither measure takes into account the number of people who watch the program but leave the room during the commercial or who look into the newspaper without ever seeing the comparable display ad. Despite these uncertainties, media planners need a number to sum the impact of a multivehicle advertising campaign, so they add the ratings of all their vehicles. The result is expressed in GRPs or Gross Ratings Points. The sum is "gross" because no allowance is made for duplication. If 50% of the households watch the TV show and the same 50% gets the newspaper, the total is 100 GRPs, even though half the audience sees neither TV nor newspaper ad.

When comparing the costs of different combinations, the ad buyer will sometimes look at "impressions" rather than rating points. Gross impressions are gross ratings expressed in actual units of individuals or households rather than as percentages of the total market. Costs of advertising are often expressed in terms of dollars per thousand impressions or CPMs. An effective tactic in selling against television is to look at the quality of those impressions. A newspaper may have a higher CPM overall than a broadcast competitor, but a lower CPM among selected, upscale demographic groups that an advertiser particularly wants to reach.

An ad salesman will stress audience composition or demographic reach, depending on which puts the buyer's needs in the best light. The difference is in the way the cross-tabs are run. If the size of the audience is small, the salesman may stress its composition, pointing out that it is largely male and upscale, if that is what the buyer wants. He may then not care—or not notice—how small it is. Composition is obtained by basing percentages on the audience, like this:

	Readers	NonReaders
Upscale	75%	50%
Downscale	25	50
	100	100

The statement that 75% of the readers are upscale may sound more impressive than the percentage based on the demographic category:

	Upscale	Downscale
Readers	60%	33%
NonReaders	40	67
	100	100

This table shows that the newspaper reaches 60% of the upscale people, which is what the rational ad buyer will want to know. And if you need convincing that these 2 tables are based on the same data, here are the raw numbers:

	Readers	NonReaders
Upscale	150	100
Downscale	50	100
	200	200

A frequent problem with multipurpose surveys is arriving at a geographic definition of the area to be studied. The newspaper industry and the broadcast industry both have their own pet definitions that are designed to emphasize their strengths. For broadcasting, the primary unit is the Area of Dominant Influence (ADI), a term coined by Arbitron, a broadcast rating company. An ADI is built from units of whole counties, and a county is assigned to the ADI whose television stations are most watched in that county. Thus, Douglas County, Kansas, is part of the Kansas City ADI, even though it is closer to Topeka, because the people in Douglas County watch more signals from Kansas City than they do from Topeka.

The fact that ADIs are built from county units is of tremendous help in linking survey data to the census because counties are highly convenient units to use when dealing with the census. The government's major statistical geographic units, the Metropolitan Statistical Areas (MSAs) and the Consolidated Statistical Areas (CSAs), also follow county lines except in New England. These areas are defined by population density and commuting patterns, and many newspaper advertising studies collect data by MSA because the same factors that contribute to the government definition of a market also usually make it the natural market for a major newspaper.

However, there is a need for a more precise definition of a newspaper's trade area that is not constrained by the requirements of ADIs or MSAs. The Audit Bureau of Circulation uses three geographic definitions. In order of ascending scope, they are:

The city zone. It starts with the political boundaries of the community in which the newspaper is published and may include some surrounding areas that have the same character.

The retail trading zone (RTZ). This larger area is defined by shopping patterns. If there are places outside the city zone containing people who shop in the city zone, those places become part of the retail trading zone.

The primary market area (PMA). Whereas the first two definitions are objective and define market areas by fixed criteria, this one is almost totally subjective. The ABC lets the publisher draw a line around his town according to his own notion of where the advertisers and the readers he wants to serve are located.

A researcher designing a readership study will generally be most interested in the PMA because that, by definition, is where the newspaper concentrates its effort. In an omnibus study, however, the advertising department may want data for the ADI in order to develop competitive ammunition to use against television. A good compromise is to sample the ADI but design an oversample of the PMA so that detailed analyses can be pursued there.

While much advertising research is based on the sample survey, there is also a long tradition of experimental research. One of the nice things about advertising research is that there is no doubt or ambiguity about the ultimate measure. The ad either sells something or it does not. The main reason that advertisers keep on advertising is that they can see the effects directly at their cash registers. And there have been some interesting experimental designs to help them find out how to achieve those effects with the most efficiency. For example, there have been split-run experiments to test the effectiveness of different kinds of ads. (Color vs. black-and-white is an example.) Coupons are a good way to measure an ad's effectiveness, because the customer carries the physical evidence to the store.

Spread of the Universal Product Code with its machine-readable symbols that are used to ring up the sale at the cash register has created a variety of opportunities for experimental research because store managers can now tell at the end of each day how many of a product they have sold and correlate that number with the level and kind of advertising. Cable television also creates some interesting opportunities. In one case, researchers sought to answer the question of whether an advertiser who wanted to increase his ad budget should spend the extra money on newspapers or television. They designed an experiment that showed an increased number of commercial messages to some cable viewers but not to others, who were used as a control. By splitting the press run, they created an experimental and a control group among newspaper readers as well (Fletcher and Bowers, 1979).

These are field experiments, meaning that they take place in fairly natural conditions. Advertising research is also conducted in the laboratory, where respondents can be asked to respond to different kinds of messages. Reader response to different kinds of editorial treatment can also be tested in the same sort of setting.

News people are sometimes suspicious of advertising research because of the unabashed economic motivation behind it. The search is not for truth for its own sake so much as for facts and figures that will support a sales argument. Yet it would be a mistake to assume that advertising research is therefore tainted. As every good salesperson knows, truth is easier to sell than falsehood, and deceptive research findings do not enjoy long life in the marketplace. Advertising researchers have a strong economic incentive to get at the truth, and, because their research is tied more directly to revenue than is editorial product research, they more often have the means to develop solid, generalizable findings. Moreover, they have increasingly sophisticated advertisers looking over their shoulders, and those advertisers have a heavy economic stake in the truth. This sort of pressure has led to some very high methodological standards and some institutional devices for enforcing them through the Advertising Research Foundation. The diligent news researcher will find that advertising researchers have much of value to share and that opportunities for cooperative effort abound.

Beyond Newspapers: Researching Videotex / 12.

The trouble with newspaper research is that you have to find out what is going on inside people's heads. And the only way to do that is to ask. How can you be sure that you are getting true answers? You can't, and newspaper research is haunted by the prospect that the respondents are putting us on—particularly when they tell us that they read the editorial page more than the comic page.

I once heard a presentation from a Canadian researcher who had gone to extreme lengths to measure the problem of misreporting by respondents. His bizarre experiment required the respondent to read a newspaper propped up on a stand in front of him while his head was kept immobile by a vise. A camera perched above the stand tracked the respondent's eye movements, and some geometric calculations were made to deduce from the eye movements what the respondent really read. He was also asked what he had read in an interview of the type conducted in readership surveys, and his answers were compared with what the camera recorded. The discrepancy between the two measures was distressingly high.

It would be nice if researchers could somehow tap directly into the user's head and make an objective record of which stories he reads, how much time he spends with them, and how deep into each story he gets. The dream is not so wild as you might think. Videotex—the latest and most sophisticated version of the electronic newspaper—can do exactly that.

Videotex is the system for delivering printed information stored in a computer to a home television screen. The user can interact with the system to make it yield whatever information he or she wants—when it is wanted. That's a nice thing for users, but it is a terrific thing for market researchers, because the same computer that manages the storage and retrieval can keep track of every page that every viewer retrieves, when it is retrieved, and even how much time elapses before the next page is retrieved. For long stories, it can count the number of pages and record exactly how deep into the story every reader—not just a sample, but every reader—was drawn.

Here is a market research problem in which the methods that were so difficult in the previous chapter become suddenly easy. There is no sampling error, and, at the household level, no measurement error. In some systems, individuals are given unique sign-on codes, and analysis at the level of the individual user is possible, but at that level there is high risk of error because there is no way to be sure that the person who signed on is still using the set at any given time, nor, for that matter, that the person signed on with his or her own code. But at the household level, the data should be free from the kinds of errors that plague sample surveys of respondents' self-reported behavior. At last, we have the capacity for direct observation of that behavior without the need to put anybody's head in a vise!

In large videotex systems, however, this may be only a theoretical capacity until computers get even bigger and faster than they are now. Data collection and storage eats up computer capacity and slows response time, which is already a problem for large systems. So the data collection is not free and operates under constraints. But it still provides capabilities that were never before available for newspaper research.

The Privacy Problem

As I write this, I cannot help noticing that the calendar on my wall reports that the year is 1984. The people who run videotex systems have been concerned with the Big Brotherish aspects of their systems, and, anticipating potential consumer resistance over that issue, they have taken steps to protect user privacy. The system that can be such a boon to market researchers could also be used to discover who lingers over listings for X-rated movies, who studies the liquor ads, and who retrieves medical advice for herpes.

The first impulse of some in this new industry is to establish procedures that destroy the identities of individual households as quickly as the records are created. This could be done by aggregating the data so that all of the numbers are kept as totals in predetermined cells. For example, the computer could tell you how many households in a predetermined demographic category retrieved the 1984 presidential election results, but not which individual households did so. And so data management systems have been designed that erase the data at the household level while preserving it in the aggregate for the previously defined cells.

Such a system certainly would solve the privacy problem, but it could deprive this developing industry of a powerful research tool. Early experience with videotex suggests that selling it will be easy, but the challenge will be to induce users to keep it once the novelty has worn off. Videotex may be subject to the same kind of churning of in-and-out users that bedevils the newspaper industry, and retention, not the original sale, will be the chief marketing problem. If so, the potential for longitudinal studies made possible by identifying individual households could be extremely important.

Newspaper studies of the retention problem have suffered from data collection problems, too-small samples, and too-short time frames. The automatic data collection of videotex could solve all of these problems, yielding very large samples over a very long time so that adequate subsamples of retainers, short-term droppers, and long-term droppers could eventually be formed. If individual household identities are retained, a researcher can go back into the data, once the identities of the households in those three retention categories have been established, to see what usage patterns tended to predict those outcomes. A finding, for example, that heavy use of neighborhood news predicts long-term retention would certainly make a system editor think twice before cutting back on neighborhood news in favor of some new and untried form of content. It would also make him or her want to experiment with increasing neighborhood news coverage until its potential for aiding retention was exhausted, and it would be a cue for the business side to use neighborhood news in its sales-promotion efforts.

This capability can be retained and privacy still respected through the use of procedural codes that will keep data on individuals from ever being made public. There is ample precedent for such codes in survey research, and they are reliable.

Finding the Right Questions

With such a tremendous capacity for getting answers, videotex researchers will face a special burden in formulating questions. The greater the number of possible research paths, the greater the risk of getting stuck on the wrong one. It will be especially important to think in terms of market needs rather than products and work backward from those needs so that the product can be fitted to them. Invention, remember, is not the mother of necessity. The parachute was invented in the fifteenth century, but nobody bought one until people started going up in hot-air balloons in the eighteenth century. It took 300 years for the invention and the necessity to come together.

It is easy to become so preoccupied with the various technical features, protocols, and delivery means of new information technology that serving human needs is often forgotten. In the 1960s, when F Street in downtown Washington, D.C., was being converted to a pedestrian mall, the designers thought kiosks would be an attractive feature, and so kiosks were built. After they were built, no one knew what to do with them, and so instead of being used to sell newspapers or postcards or flowers to passersby, they were used for many years to store brooms and shovels for street maintenance crews. The device, not the need, had come first.

I thought of those unused kiosks one winter when a snowstorm forced the closing of schools in my town. In the early morning, I tuned the radio to the local station and waited patiently until the announcer got around to announcing the closing of my children's schools. Only afterward did it occur to me to try the channel reserved for school announcements on the town's state-of-the-art cable TV system. Instead of listening to fifteen minutes of bad music while waiting for the announcement, I could have gone straight to the source. Out of curiosity, I flipped on the school channel to see how the announcement was handled and discovered to my surprise that it wasn't there. The channel still displayed the school lunch menu and the exam schedule that would have been in effect if school had been held that day. The moral of this anecdote is that it takes more than an engineering device to make things happen. There must be a need, and there must be people and organizations to see that the device is applied toward meeting that need. Finding the links between the need and the device is the job of market research.

The Economics of Videotex

The economic pressures in favor of videotex appear to be strong. For a variety of information-related industries, it promises cheap, reliable delivery of information, and the conversion of many variable costs to fixed costs. The latter point is so important that it deserves some explanation.

When a newspaper succeeds in increasing its circulation, it does not need, within certain limits, to increase the size of the staff that produces the editorial content or sells the advertising. These costs are fixed and have to be paid whether circulation grows, declines, or stays the same. That is good news for the successful publisher.

The bad news is that certain other costs are variable and will increase with circulation. The costs of newsprint and ink will rise in proportion to circulation. So will the costs of transporting those additional newspapers to their readers. In most businesses, savings in variable costs are valued more than savings in fixed costs because the variable costs can be barriers to growth.

Broadcasting has always had this key advantage over print: nearly all of its costs are fixed. A station in a growing market can serve additional customers with no additional expense for the electricity that it takes to send out the signal. The appeal of electronic publishing for the newspaper industry is that the variable costs of ink, paper, and transportation disappear in favor of a better equation weighted much more heavily toward fixed costs. It has long been a source of frustration in the newspaper industry that technology's advances have all come in the less important area of fixed costs at the front end of the production process while doing nothing for the variable back end.

Other industries see the same sorts of potential savings, and one of the research questions should explore the potential for linking their needs to services that a newspaper company can provide. Banks can reduce their variable personnel costs and serve more customers without adding tellers if videotex brings banking services directly to the home. Electronic banking also has some promise of reducing the period when funds are being processed and are temporarily unavailable, providing yet another economic incentive for banks to try the new technology.

The Value-Added Concept

All of the business incentives may mean little if there is no corresponding consumer incentive to use the new technology. For consumers to pay money for these services, uses and gratifications must be provided that are not available at less cost or greater convenience from other sources. In analyzing this problem, it helps to think of ways that the new information technology might add value to the information it distributes.

One form of value is timeliness. Instant gratification is probably worth money to some consumers. Information in a videotex system can be updated constantly so that information delivery need not be tied to the 24-hour delivery cycle of a newspaper or the different but still regular cycles of other media. A useful side effect of the timeliness value is the improvement in accuracy. As a newspaper reporter, I often wished that I had some magic device that would enable me to enter every subscriber's home and erase some embarrassing error I had made in that day's paper. Videotex, of course, can do exactly that.

Another way to add value is through the sheer volume of material collected and stored. Most of us at one time or another have experienced the frustration of wanting a newspaper or magazine article and finding that the publication in question had been thrown away. Even if we had the storage space to save a five-year supply of newspapers and magazines, the problem of retrieving the desired information from that volume of material would probably discourage us. Videotex solves both the storage and the retrieval problems. Consumer access to back issues of newspapers with keyword indexing is already becoming available in this country, and it has existed for several years in Toronto, where the *Globe and Mail* has a successful electronic newspaper library.

The third way that value is added is through the interactive capability of the system that makes convenient transactional services possible. If consumers in their living rooms can perform transactions that normally require leaving home, finding a parking space, and standing in line, they will save time and money, and the service could quickly become an economic necessity. Helping businesses design transactional services in a way that takes advantage of these capabilities of videotex is an important function for marketing research.

Current Videotex Research

The fragments of publicly released research results so far provide conflicting indications. British reports on the use of Prestel reveal little interest in using videotex to retrieve large volumes of data. Where news stories last more than one page, viewers are reluctant to penetrate beyond the first page or two. On the other hand, in the Knight-Ridder test with AT&T in Coral Gables, Florida, a greater variety of user patterns was reported. Some users paged all the way through fairly lengthy news stories while others were content with less detail. The difference may be due in part to the attractive way in which the Knight-Ridder news stories were edited and packaged. But the fact that the British pay for their information by the frame may also help account for the difference. Users in the Coral Gables experiment paid nothing.

The early experiments also suggest that the appetite for highly specialized media, already discovered by newspapers, might be efficiently satisfied by videotex. With storage and retrieval from large volumes of data no longer a problem, it might become feasible to do for urban neighborhoods what country weeklies used to do on rural routes. When my parents drove with my brother and me to Sunday dinners at my grandmother's farm near Linn, Kansas, my grandmother, knowing I aspired to be a journalist, always insisted that I write a few lines on the visit for the *Linn-Palmer Record.* James K. Batten of Knight-Ridder Newspapers calls this micronews, and it can be brought down to an intensely local level with videotex. In the South Florida Viewtron system, which became operational in the fall of 1983, a user could check a specific, narrowly defined location on the map for news of a crime or a real estate sale.

For researchers, the question is how detailed this information can get for the costs of collection to be justified by the contribution to retention. The reporting task has not been automated. The work of editing and formatting information must also be done with human brains and hands. It is easy to become so fascinated with the technical achievement of storing and distributing information that the need for an editor is forgotten, but someone has to decide what message to make available to whom and in what form. When the snowstorm closed the schools in my town, it was the lack of an editor that kept the cable system from giving me that information.

Experimentation with videotex is likely to produce a variety of styles. One option is to shove material into the system wholesale without much editing because it will soon be outdated anyway. The contrasting style is to recast all of the information into crisp, tight phrases that make it easy for a user to absorb the content with a minimum of effort. Market research is needed to compare the benefits of these two approaches with their costs. The way frames are linked together is crucial: the user must be able to progress from one frame to another in the manner that fits individual information needs. A skilled editor can provide multiple linkages and clear directions on each frame so that the user is never left at a dead end with no idea of what to do next. Research on the different navigation systems can guide editors on the best ways to guide their users.

Careful editing makes printed information on the TV screen easy on the eyes. Writers who are used to print media tend to pack the information tightly onto the screen so as not to waste any of the space. But, since that space is used over and over again, it is not such a scarce commodity as to require conservation. Experienced videotex operators are learning to keep plenty of blank space surrounding the words to make reading easy and to employ color for contrast.

These factors are important, but even more important is giving videotex a personality. Market research can test whether that personality is seen as friendly or threatening, warm or aloof.

Only when market research has helped the sellers of videotex services to discover the consumer needs that they can satisfy will they be able to define for themselves what business they are in. At first glance, it looks like the information business, but it may prove to be something else. Hal Jurgensmeyer of the University of Miami recognized years ago that a newspaper gets most of its revenue because it is able to help advertisers influence customers who patronize them. To fill that role, a home information system needs to be more than a medium for transactions or a tollgate for information buyers and sellers. It needs to establish itself as a presence in the community, to help the community define and improve itself, and even to create communities where none existed before. This presence makes it credible and desirable as an advertising medium.

Some observers of the videotex scene believe that consumer demand will not be sufficient to support it, at least in the beginning, and that its main promise is in business applications. Some Prestel operators in England came to that conclusion, but they quickly learned that business and personal use can be more difficult to distinguish than was supposed. Business users developed the habit of making personal use of videotex on the job—to find theater listings or search the classifieds, for example—and home users found ways to use the home terminals for work. There are bound to be other surprises, but imaginative market research can reduce their number and magnitude.

CONCLUSIONS / IV

Some Things We've Learned / from Research / 13.

Many years ago, when newspaper managers were first becoming interested in market research, I was asked to speak to an editors' meeting about substantive wisdom gleaned from research. "Give us a list," said Derick Daniels, the presiding editor, "of twenty to twenty-five things that we know for sure because of research."

I stopped and thought. "Give me a week," I said, "and I might be able to come up with three."

Those editors got their three rules, and as time went by I added to the list, eventually increasing it to eight homilies. But I was never able to expand beyond that without straying from substantive advice of the do-this-and-not-that variety. And on some days, I'm not too sure about these eight.

Here they are, nevertheless: eight generic rules for editing a newspaper that ought to apply to most newspapers most of the time, all derived from research findings.

Rule 1: Make Television Work for You.

For a long time, editors acted as though television would go away if they ignored it. Some still do. Writing about television, according to this view, is giving aid to the enemy and encouraging people to watch the tube when they should be reading their newspapers.

When editors did pay attention to TV, it was often for the wrong reason. At one newspaper I know about, the city desk assigned an assistant city editor to watch the local news and schedule stories that appeared there for less play than stories that the newspaper had exclusively. That was wrong.

What research tells us about television is that it is not going to go away and that it creates interests in the public that, if followed up by careful editing, can drive people to the newspaper. Here's an example.

When "The Day After" was shown on network television on November

20, 1983, a large portion of its 100 million viewers stayed tuned to watch a panel of experts talk about avoiding nuclear war. One of the experts was Robert McNamara, the former defense secretary under President Kennedy, and he said he had a list of fifteen things that this government could do right now, unilaterally, to reduce the risk of nuclear holocaust. As often happens with television, there wasn't time to follow up on that intriguing scrap, and the show ended without McNamara unloading even one of those fifteen proposals. Millions of viewers went to bed that night with a question on their minds that only a well-edited print medium could answer.

I'm sure some newspapers did follow up on McNamara's thoughts, although none of those that I read that week did. *Newsweek,* however, produced a terrific follow with a cover story and a sidebar on McNamara's proposals—by then expanded to eighteen—in its issue of December 5. That is heads-up reporting, but newspaper people too often miss chances like that because they mistakenly assume that what TV does is irrelevant to what they do.

There are other ways to take advantage of television. A newspaper should provide high-quality viewing guides that help the reader plan his time. This is especially important with the advent of cable, whose operators do not do a good job of letting their subscribers know what is available. When a newspaper jumps in to do that job, it is building a strong bond between itself and the reader.

Here's another way. Assign one of the clever writers, the sort who eventually gets a local page column, to write about television in a relaxed and rambling way that also shares the writer's philosophy of life, however bizarre. When you are writing about television, you are writing about the one thing that binds the audience together in a common experience more than any other.

Rule 2: Emphasize Specialized Content.

I like this rule because it is counterintuitive, meaning that what most editors feel in their guts is just its opposite. When space is short, they tend to use the precious remaining columns on material with the broadest possible appeal. But that is wasteful because the broad-based appeal tends to reach people at a low level of intensity.

The high-intensity items are often narrowly addressed ones, as any editor who has ever tried to drop a crossword puzzle knows. A newspaper audience is a mosaic of many small special but intense interests, and if you cut back on those interests when space is short, you stand to lose more net readership than a cutback of more general material would.

This doesn't mean you can throw out all the broad-based material in favor of crossword puzzles, but you can trim the broad area without much damage because much of the material there is cumulative and repetitive.

Rule 3: Make the Paper Efficient As an Information Retrieval Device.

John LeGates of the Harvard University Program on Information Resources Policy told a meeting of ANPA directors about a technology that would "carry 30 million bits of information, weigh less than three pounds, handle both text and graphics, be completely portable, be accessible in any order, operate 24 hours a day, cost less than 25 cents a connect hour, and be mostly paid for by someone else." He was talking, of course, about the daily newspaper.

To make it work, however, you need to label, anchor, and index. The labels help the reader find what he or she wants. Putting the same features in the same places keeps the paper familiar and reassuring. And a good index will help even the new reader to navigate through the newsprint. The designers of USA *Today* knew exactly what they were doing when they formatted that paper so tightly that anyone who has read it once knows exactly how to use it the next time he or she picks it up.

A few papers have carried indexing even to the point of indexing the advertising by product line: an excellent idea, serving readers and advertisers alike. Some advertisers may not like it because they think it reduces traffic through the newspaper. But the traditional notion that readers invariably start on page one and go straight through the paper may be unsound, particularly for larger papers. The readers of one large paper I know about have shown a bewildering variety of traffic patterns, with many putting page one fairly low on their personal priority lists.

Rule 4: Do Something for the Kids.

Habits developed in childhood affect what people do as adults. One of the main benefits of the Newspaper in Education program has been that it puts the paper in the hands of children from homes where it is not normally present, giving them a better chance of being readers when they grow up.

Comics help, but there should be more daily features aimed at kids, preferably in a section that can be pulled or clipped out. That market segment tends to be overlooked because national advertisers have not been turned on to newspapers as a medium for kids. That should be corrected.

Rule 5: Don't Be Afraid of Media Overkill.

People use newspapers to learn more about what they have heard elsewhere. They have seldom heard as much as the editor, so the editor is more likely than the typical reader to sense a surfeit of news on a given topic.

The general rule to follow is that the more other media are playing a story, the harder newspapers should work to cover it, too. People will snap it up long after the point where the editor gags. Remember the death of Elvis Presley? Some papers dropped the story after the second day. Others rode it, hell for leather, for weeks. When a story is big in the other media, grit your teeth, and keep piling it on.

Rule 6: Remember the Importance of National and International News.

Editors love local stories because that's where they have the most control over the amount and nature of the coverage. But TV has had the effect of bringing the whole world closer together.

The textbook aphorism that a cat fight on Main Street is worth more than a thousand riot deaths in Aleppo no longer holds. TV is that cat fight, and it brings Aleppo to us all. Believe the research respondents when they say that national news and international news are high on their list of wants.

Rule 7: Design the Paper to Sell Itself in the Home.

Just getting the paper into the home is no longer enough. Circulation no longer counts as much as the number who "read yesterday," and a distressing number of people whose households have the newspaper available turn up missing when the read-yesterday roll is taken.

Street editions are designed with the impulse reader in mind. Attractive home-delivery editions might stimulate use of the paper once it is delivered. The back of section pages may be too good for advertisers if they can be packed with news summaries and attracting standing short features to entice everyone in the household to get some ink on his or her hands.

Rule 8: Forget the Hard-Core Nonreader.

Another counterintuitive rule. An editor will look at a survey that says 90 percent of his audience reads the paper at least some of the time and start worrying about the remaining 10. Forget them. They are uneducated and unaffluent, and you won't miss them. The key to increasing net, read-yesterday readership is not the nonreader but the sometime reader who is churning at the margin. The doable task, the important task, is to slow the rate of churn.

Look for strategies to retard the churn, to keep the less frequent readers coming back for more. Don't sneer at serial comics because mostly older readers follow them. There are a few serials that are followed by younger readers, and they can make the paper more of a daily habit.

I like this rule best of all, because its logic says that newspapers should be made better. Period. Improve your paper for the readers you already have, and you will make it more attractive to the churning ones as well. As Alvah Chapman has said, "We ought to farm as well as we know how."

How to Evaluate a / Research Department / Appendix

A newspaper research department can serve a great variety of functions, and there is no well-defined industry standard—as there is for most other departments of a newspaper—for just what it ought to do. Most departments have grown on an ad hoc basis. Some are run by professional researchers, others by people who have done a variety of jobs on the newspaper but have not had formal research training.

The following checklist arranges the functions of a research department in ascending order of difficulty. Generally, a department that can do any given task on the list is capable of performing lesser-ranked tasks. There is only a rough correlation between the size of a paper and the capabilities of its research department. The circulation size at which a newspaper could reasonably be expected to have a research department with each level of capability is also indicated.

Level 1: Desk research. Maintain a library of census data for your market along with other published materials from state and local planning agencies that contain descriptive materials on the market. Collect and review the main sources for findings on editorial research: *Journalism Quarterly, Newspaper Research Journal, ANPA News Research Bulletin,* and publications of the Newspaper Advertising Bureau, particularly those generated by the Newspaper Readership Project. Help management to draw inferences for strategic decisions based on integrating the generic findings from these publications with the specifics from your market. A newspaper with circulation of 25,000 can make this at least a part-time function for someone who may have other responsibilities, such as promotion.

Level 2: Contracting with research suppliers. Solicit and evaluate proposals from research suppliers for projects designed to meet specific management problems. Advise top management on the choice of a contractor. Monitor the performance of the contract and evaluate the results. Assist management with the interpretation of the findings and development of policy decisions based on the findings. While not every newspaper with at least 50,000 circulation will have a person with this regular responsibility, it is reasonable to expect it at this size.

Level 3: Writing detailed research specifications and bidding them out. At this level, the research manager is less passive in the process and goes to the suppliers with much more specific assignments in mind. At Level 2, the research manager explains a problem and asks the supplier how to handle it. At Level 3, the newspaper's research staff knows how it wants the problem handled and can state its needs quite specifically. This makes competitive bidding much more practical because all the contenders for the job, if the specifications are tight enough, are bidding on the same thing. Expect this capability as circulation approaches 100,000.

Level 4: Conducting secondary analysis. Formal research training is a must at this level. Research is now more than a one-person operation, and at least one person on the staff can use one of the statistical analysis computer programs, such as SAS or SPSS, preferably installed on the newspaper's own computer. When specifications for research projects are written, one of the requirements is for delivery of a codebook and raw data tape so that the staff can continue to wring information out of the data after the supplier has left the scene. These data can often be used to solve new problems not foreseen when the project was first planned. Newspapers of greater than 100,000 circulation should be able to support this capability.

Level 5: Research design and execution, except for field work. At this level a marketing researcher can perform all of the creative tasks involved in a research project. The supplier is given a sample design—or even an actual sample—and a questionnaire, and it returns a data tape and a codebook. The newspaper's researchers go on from there, performing all of the analysis and interpretation. This capability will not be used all of the time, but the fact that it exists makes the research department much stronger as a consumer and interpreter of research. Maintaining it becomes feasible as circulation size approaches 200,000.

Level 6: Total design and execution. Newspapers at this level maintain their own field operations and can do most things that commercial suppliers do. Some even become commercial suppliers to other newspapers and general business clients. They may still hire outside researchers for projects where an objective investigator is needed to maintain credibility with advertisers, but they know as much about the process as the people with whom they contract, which gives them good negotiating and supervisory position. This capability is rare in newspaper research departments, and, when it is found, it is generally in newspapers beyond the 200,000 circulation level.

Bibliography

Batten, James K. Remarks to Annual Meeting of the Southern Newspaper Publishers' Association. Boca Raton, Fla., 1983.

Belden, Joe, and John Schweitzer. "The Effect of Distance on News Appeal." Belden Research Seminar, Dallas. 1978.

Berg, Thomas L. *Mismarketing*. New York: Doubleday, 1970.

Bing, Gordon. *Corporate Acquisitions*. Houston: Gulf Publishing Company, 1980.

Bogart, Leo. "Psychology on a Large Scale: The Study of Consumption." *American Psychologist*, November 1973.

————. *Press and Public*. New York: Lawrence Erlbaum Associates, 1981.

Brown, Chip. "Baltimore's *Sun* Faces a New Day." *Washington Post*, 7 March 1982.

Burroughs, Elise. "Modern Marketing Makes Its Mark." *presstime*, December 1981.

Clark, Ruth. *Changing Needs of Changing Readers: A Qualitative Study of the New Social Contract Between Newspaper Editors and Readers*. Reston, Virginia: American Society of Newspaper Editors, 1979.

Cobbey, Robin F., and Maxwell E. McCombs. "Using a Decision Model to Evaluate Newspaper Features Systematically." *Journalism Quarterly*, Autumn 1979.

Davis, Robert. *The Public Impact of Science on the Mass Media*. Ann Arbor: Survey Research Center, 1958.

Fallows, James. "The New Immigrants." *The Atlantic*, November 1983.

Fletcher, Alan D., and Thomas A. Bowers. *Fundamentals of Advertising Research*. Columbus, Ohio: Grid Publishing Company, 1979.

Greenberger, Martin, Matthew A. Crenson, and Brian L. Crissey. *Models in the Policy Process*. New York: Russell Sage Foundation, 1976.

Haskins, Jack. "The Editorial Mix: One Solution to a Magazine Editor's Dilemma." *Journalism Quarterly*, Fall 1965.

Hirt, Paul S. *Newspaper Marketing: A Time for Reappraisal?* Reston, Virginia: International Newspaper Promotion Association, 1983.

Lane, Robert E. "The Decline of Politics and Ideology in a Knowledgeable Society." *The American Journal of Sociology*, 71: 591, 1966.

Lipset, Seymour Martin. Quoted in *Knight-Ridder News Research Letter*, Miami, Fla., April 1979.

Maisel, Richard. "The Decline of Mass Media." *Public Opinion Quarterly*, Summer 1973.

McCombs, Maxwell E. "Mass Media in the Marketplace." *Journalism Monographs*, August 1972.

————. "What to Drop and What to Keep? A Scientific Procedure for Evaluating Standing Features." *ANPA News Research Report No. 4*, July 1977.

Miller, Warren E., and Teresa E. Levitin. *Leadership and Change: The New Politics and the American Electorate*. Cambridge: Winthrop Publishers, 1976.

National Opinion Research Center. *General Social Surveys, 1972–1983: Cumulative Codebook*. Storrs, Connecticut: The Roper Center, 1983.

Newspaper Advertising Bureau. *Two Dimensions of News: Interest and Importance Ratings of the Editorial Content of the American Press*. New York: NAB, 1978.

Nunn, Clyde Z. "Newspapers with Separate Editorial Managements Have Higher Household Penetration." *ANPA News Research Report No. 17*, December 1978.

Robinson, John P., and Leo W. Jeffres. "A Cohort Analysis Perspective on 'The Death of Print.'" Unpublished. 1979.

Rogers, Everett M., and F. Floyd Shoemaker. *Communication of Innovations: A Cross-Cultural Approach*. New York: The Free Press, 1971.

Schramm, Wilbur. "Channels and Audiences." In *Handbook of Communication*. Ed. Ithielde Sola Pool. Chicago: Rand-McNally, 1973.

Stewart, David W. "The Application and Misapplication of Factor Analysis in Marketing Research." *Journal of Marketing Research*, February 1981.

Surmanek, Jim. *Media Planning: A Quick and Easy Guide*. Chicago: Crain Books, 1980.

Toffler, Alvin. *Future Shock*. New York: Random House, 1970.

———. *The Third Wave*. New York: William Morrow and Company, 1980.

Tukey, John. *Exploratory Data Analysis*. Reading, Massachusetts: Addison-Wesley, 1977.

Verba, Sidney, and Norman Nie. *Participation in America*. New York: Harper and Row, 1972. Data collected in 1967 and archived at National Opinion Research Center, University of Chicago.

Weaver, David H., John C. Schweitzer, and Gerald C. Stone. "Content, Appearance and Circulation: An Analysis of Individual Newspaper Characteristics." *ANPA News Research Report No. 2*, April 1977.

Wegner, Daniel M. "Hidden Brain-Damage Scale." *American Psychologist*, February 1979.

Wells, William D. "Group Interviewing." In *Handbook of Marketing Research*. Ed. Robert Ferber. New York: McGraw-Hill, 1974.

General Index

Action-oriented research, 59
Action standards, 30–31
ADI. *See* Television advertising, Area of Dominant Influence
Advertisers
  and duplication of audience, 126, 130–31
  and market domination, 9
  short-term satisfaction of, 3
Advertising research
  audience composition, 142–43
  circulation information, use of, 134
  color usage, 63–64
  cumulative readership (cume), 138–39, 140
  experimental research in, 63–64, 144–45
  geographic definition of study area, 143–44
  gross impressions, 142
  increases in, 23
  intermedia comparisons, 139–44
  interviewing techniques, 135–37, 138
  measures for, 134–36
  newspaper research and, 136–37, 145
  ratings, use of, 141–42
  "reach," 137–38
  See also Television advertising
All-day newspapers, 121, 132
American Newspaper Publishers Association News Research Center (ANPA), 26, 33

Baby Boomers, 14–22
Baltimore Sun, 6–7
Boston Globe, 65, 121

Census data, 32
Chapman, Alvah, 161
Charitable foundations, 6
Charlotte News, 120
Charlotte Observer, 120
Chicago Daily News, 132
Chicago Sun-Times, 132
Children's features, 66, 159–60
Circulation
  and advertising research, 134
  evaluation of, 54–57

and page-one design, 64–65
and reach-cost ratio, 128–29, 130
in second-paper situations, 123, 125–26
See also Penetration
Cluster-analysis, 31–32
Comic-strip problem
  audience attraction, 115–16
  classification of strips, 110–13
  "comic to drop" decision, 118–19
  decision making under constraint, 109
  overlapping readership, 116–18
  readership concerns, 111–18
  space concerns, 112
Communications, 24–25, 31
"Compunications" revolution, 13
Consumer diaries, 31
Consumer information features, 43, 44
Consumers, editorial power of, 6
Content studies, 38, 41, 42–46, 56–62, 65–66, 73, 76–77
Correlation coefficient, 49–50
Correlation matrix, 40
Cross-lagged correlation, 68
Cross-tabulation, 25
Cumulative readership (cume), 138–39, 140

Dacia study, 70–76
Daniels, Derick, 157
Davies, Michael, 121
Dayparts, 140
Decision making, 24, 31, 109
Delivery service, 73, 75–76
Des Moines Register and Tribune, 121
Diffusion theory, 18–21
Duplication of audience, 126–28, 130–31

Editorial operations, 3–4
Editors
  personal views of, 7–8
  rules for, 157–61
Electronic publishing. *See* Videotex
Entrepreneurial companies, ix
Experimental research
  in advertising research, 63–64, 144–45
  on circulation, 64–65

Authors Cited

WITHDRAWN
FROM
UNIVERSITY OF PENNSYLVANIA
LIBRARIES